STATISM II

Solemnly Warn Them

Also From Tanglewood Publishing

STATISM: THE SHADOWS OF ANOTHER NIGHT

THE CONFESSIONS OF OUR FAITH (PROOFS CITED)

THE CONFESSIONS OF OUR FAITH (LEATHER EDITION)

THE CONFESSIONS OF OUR FAITH (ARABIC EDITION)

WESTMINSTER DAILY DEVOTIONAL

CREATED BY GOD - PURCHASED BY CHRIST (VOL. 1, STUDIES IN THE WESTMINSTER SHORTER CATECHISM)

REASON FOR HEAVEN

LIVING RIGHT - LIVING WELL (VOL. 2, STUDIES IN THE WESTMINSTER SHORTER CATECHISM)

A GUIDE TO PHONETICS AND ARTICULATION

THE CONFESSIONS OF OUR FAITH WITH ESV PROOFS

COMMUNION WITH OUR GOD (VOL. 3, STUDIES IN THE WESTMINSTER SHORTER CATECHISM)

REFLECTIONS ON THE 7 LAST WORDS OF CHRIST

SILENT NO MORE

EASY RESEARCH PAPER

KILLING JESUS OF NAZARETH

JOURNEY OF A LIFETIME

JULIA LEARNS HOW TO MARRY WISELY

WESTMINSTER SHORTER CATECHISM: BIBLE STUDY AND COMMENTARY

STATISM II

Solemnly Warn Them

Edited by Charlie Rodriguez

TANGLEWOOD
PUBLISHING

Best of the Best in All Academic Disciplines

STATISM II
Solemnly Warn Them

Cover Design by Christy Rodriguez
Book Design and Layout by Mieke Moller

Printed in the United States of America

Contents

Statism

"Socialism is a philosophy of failure, the creed of ignorance, and the gospel of envy, its inherent virtue is the equal sharing of misery."

WINSTON CHURCHILL

Statism

The Biggest Concern for the Future of the Church in America

by R.C. Spoul

"A decree went out from Caesar Augustus that all the world should be registered...." In Luke 2, the well-known passage introducing the nativity story, the title accorded to the Roman emperor is Caesar Augustus. Had this census been mandated earlier under the monarchy of Julius Caesar, the Scripture would read: "A decree went out from Julius Caesar...." Had Octavian followed the model of Julius, he would have called himself Octavianus Caesar, and then the text would read: "A decree went out from Octavianus Caesar...." But we note Octavius' explicit change of his personal name to the title Caesar Augustus. This indicates the emerging dimension of the emperor cult in Rome, by which those who were elevated to the role of emperor were worshiped as deities. To be called "august" would mean to be clothed with supreme dignity, to which is owed the reverence given to the sacred. The elevation of the emperor in Rome to this kind of status was the ancient zenith of statism.

About thirty years ago, I shared a taxi cab in St. Louis with Francis Schaeffer. I had known Dr. Schaeffer for many years, and he had been instrumental in helping us begin our ministry in Ligonier, Pennsylvania, in 1971. Since our time together in St. Louis was during the twilight of Schaeffer's career, I posed this question to him: "Dr. Schaeffer, what is your biggest concern for the future of the church in America?" Without hesitation, Dr. Schaeffer turned to me and spoke one word: "Statism." Schaeffer's biggest concern at that point in his life was that the citizens of the United States were beginning to invest their country with supreme authority, such that the free nation of America would become one that would be dominated by a philosophy of the supremacy of the state.

In statism, we see the suffix "ism," which indicates a philosophy or worldview. A decline from statehood to statism happens when the government is perceived as or claims to be the ultimate reality. This reality then replaces God as the supreme entity upon which human existence depends.

In the nineteenth century, Hegel argued in his extensive and complex study of Western history that progress represents the unfolding in time and space of the absolute Idea (Hegel's vague understanding of God), which would reach its apex in the creation of the Prussian state. The assumption that Hegel made in the nineteenth century was made before the advent of Hitler's Third Reich, Stalin's Russia, and Chairman Mao's communist China. These nations reached an elevation of statism never dreamed of by Hegel in his concept of the Prussian state.

In America, we have a long history of valuing the concept of the separation of church and state. This idea historically referred to a division of labors between the church and the civil magistrate. However, initially both the church and the state were seen as entities ordained by God and subject to His governance. In that sense, the state was considered to be an entity that was "under God." What has happened in the past few decades is the obfuscation of this original distinction between church and state, so that today the language we hear of separation of church and state, when carefully exegeted, communicates the idea of the separation of the state from God. In this sense, it's not merely that the state declares independence from the church, it also declares independence from God and presumes itself to rule with autonomy.

The whole idea of a nation under God has been challenged again and again, and we have seen the exponential growth of government in our land, particularly the federal government, so that the government now virtually engulfs all of life. Where education once was under the direction of local authorities, it now is controlled and directed by federal legislation. The economy that once was driven by the natural forces of the market has now come under the strict control of the federal government, which not only regulates the economy, but considers itself responsible for controlling it. Where we have seen the largest measure of the loss of liberty is with respect to the function of the church. Though the church is still somewhat tolerated in America (in a way it was not tolerated in Mao's Red China and under Stalin), it is tolerated only when it remains outside of the public square. In other words, the church has been relegated to a status not unlike that given to the native Americans, where the tribes were allowed to continue to exist as long as they functioned safely on a reservation, outside of any significant influence on the government. So although the church has not been banished completely by the statism that has emerged in America, it has been effectively banished from the public square.

Throughout the history of the Christian church, Christianity has always stood over against all forms of statism. Statism is the natural and ultimate enemy to Christianity because it involves a usurpation of the reign of God. If Francis Schaeffer was right - and each year that passes makes his prognosis seem all the more accurate - it means that the church and the nation face a serious crisis in our day. In the final analysis, if statism prevails in America, it will mean not only the death of our religious freedom, but also the death of the state itself. We face perilous times where Christians and all people need to be vigilant about the rapidly encroaching elevation of the state to supremacy.

Robert Charles Sproul is an American Reformed theologian, author, and pastor. He is the founder and chairman and can be heard daily on the Renewing Your Mind radio broadcast in the United States and internationally.

Permission to reprint granted to Fortress Book Service by Ligonier Ministries

A Prayer for Our Time

"I will answer them before they even call to me.
While they are still talking about their needs,
I will go ahead and answer their prayers"

Isaiah 65:24, NLT

A Prayer for Our Time

by Michael A. Milton, Ph.D.

O Lord our God, good Father, Eternal Refuge, One-True-King, and only Provider and Sustainer of life and liberty, You demonstrated unknown, unfathomable love and iridescent heavenly glory with, in, and through the suffering and death of Your Son, our Savior, Jesus Christ, upon Calvary's cross.

Grant faith for Your people in this exceptional hour of history, when bloated state governments, beast-like, gorge on the inalienable rights and God-given liberties of Your specially created beings, denying the dignity and imago Dei of the same and trampling on precious rights secured with the blood of heroes.

Hear our plea and answer our prayer offered in proper humility and utter dependence for grace beneath suffering, for effective Gospel witness through tribulations, for spiritual and confessional unity amidst organizational and historical diversity within the Church.

We, who live in these dire days of cultural deconstruction and unprecedented approbation of that which You call sin, may recall that we are not the first to encounter trials. We have been warned that such trails would come, and that we might suffer rightly in all righteousness, and not in sins of violence, complaining, unbelieving, or kicking against the goad.

As meek disciples of Jesus we must pray for those who persecute us, trusting that we are more than conquerors through these very things. Endue Your people with courage, remembering that You, O Father, have ordained whatsoever comes to pass, yet without sin, that our prayers are answered even before we call.

Help us to pray confidently as we pray through the name of our Lord Jesus Christ, who reigns with You and the Holy Spirit, One God, now and forevermore. Amen

Michael A. Milton, Ph.D. (University of Wales, Trinity Saint David's College) is a Presbyterian minister (PCA), educator, author, public servant, and musician. The president of Faith for Living, Inc. and the D. James Kennedy Institute, he is the speaker on the national broadcast, Truth That Transforms.

From **Annotations
on a Letter That
Changed the World
from a Birmingham Jail**

*"Let justice roll down like waters,
and righteousness like an every-flowing stream"*

AMOS 5:24

An Unfulfilled Longing:
To Hear, "Integration is Morally Right
Because the Negro Is Your Brother"

From *Annotations on a Letter*
That Changed the World
from a Birmingham Jail

---

by Peter Lillback

(Providence Forum Press, King of Prussia, PA, pp. 85-91)

D r. King: *I have heard numerous religious leaders of the South call upon their worshippers to comply with a desegregation decision because it is the law, but I have longed to hear white ministers say follow this decree because integration is morally right and the Negro is your brother. In the midst of blatant injustices inflicted upon the Negro. I have watched white churches stand on the sideline and merely mouth pious irrelevancies and sanctimonious trivialities. In the midst of a mighty struggle to rid our nation of racial injustice, I have heard so many ministers say, "Those are social issues with which the gospel has no real concern,: and I have watched so many churches commit themselves to a completely other-worldly religion which made a strange distinction between body and soul, the sacred and the secular.*

So here we are moving toward the exit of the twentieth century with a religious community largely adjusted to the status quo, standing as a taillight behind other community agencies rather than a headlight leading men to higher levels of justice.

Dr. Lillback: Dr. King's complaint here touches on an important debate within the Presbyterian tradition. There has been a substantial difference of perspective between those who view the church's primary calling to be spiritual in focus, "the Spirituality of the Church" and those who hold to a measured degree of activism or "prophetic witness" by the Church in the social and political arena. The Southern Presbyterian tradition emphasized the spirituality of the church viewpoint. One of its leading Civil War era theologians, James Henley Thornwell, affirmed the thesis "Whether slavery exists or not is a question which exclusively belongs to the State". In this context he argued, "We have no right, as a church, to enjoin as a duty, or to condemn it as a sin. . . .The social, civil, political problems connected with this great subject transcend our sphere. as God has not entrusted to his Church the organization of society, the construction of Government, nor the allotment of individuals to their various stations." (Address to the Presbyterian Church in the Confederate States of America, 1861.)

The Northern Presbyterian tradition has differed from Thornwell's view of the spirituality of the Church and has been greatly impacted by the theological position of Charles Hodge. Hodge was in the Northern Presbyterian tradition having been born in Pennsylvania and served for many years as Professor of Systematic Theology at Princeton in the 1800's. Early in his career, he was supportive of the position that defended the legitimacy of slavery, but by 1846, he openly declared that slavery was morally wrong:

Slavery is a heinous crime; it degrades human beings into things; it forbids marriages; it destroys domestic relations; it separates parents and children, husbands and wives; it legalizes what God forbids, and forbids what God enjoins; it keeps its victims in ignorance even of the gospel; it denies labor its wages, subject the persons, the virtue, and the happiness of many to the caprice of one; it involves the violation of all social rights and duties, and therefore is the greatest of social crimes. It is as much as any man's character for sense, honesty or religion is worth, to insist that a distinction must here be made; that we must discriminate between slavery and its separable adjuncts; between the relationship itself and the abuse of it; between the possession of power and unjust exerciser of it. Let any man in some portions of our country, in England, in Scotland, or

Ireland, attempt to make such distinctions, and see with what an outburst of indignation he will be overwhelmed. It is just so in the present case. (Charles Hodge, The Princeton Review, April 1846).

Furthermore, in his Systematic Theology, he rejected the theory that blacks were not fully human, and thus not made in the image of God, one of the arguments that was used by some to justify slavery:

Whenever we meet a man, no matter of what name or nation, we not only find that he has the same nature with ourselves; that he has the same organs, the same senses, the same instincts, the same feelings, the same faculties, the same understanding, will, and conscience, and the same capacity for religious culture, but that he has the same guilty and polluted nature, and needs the same redemption. Christ died for all men, and we are commanded to preach the gospel to every creature under heaven. Accordingly, nowhere on the face of the earth are men to be found who do not need the gospel or who are not capable of becoming partakers of the blessings which it offers. (Charles Hodge, Systematic Theology, 1872, Volume II, pp. 90-91).

Moreover, the Northern Presbyterian tradition has affirmed that it is appropriate for the church to address the civil magistrate in moral issues raised by governmental actions. For example, Westminster Theological Seminary Professor John Murray, a member of the Orthodox Presbyterian Church, born in Scotland and trained at Princeton, called for the Church to speak into the moral arena inclusive of the state, while being careful not to become a political entity:

When the laws are proposed or enacted that are contrary to the Word of God, it is the duty of the church in proclamation and in official pronouncement to oppose and condemn them. . .It is misconception of what is involved in the proclamation of the whole counsel of God to suppose or plead that the church has no concern with the political sphere. The Church is concerned with every sphere and is obligated to proclaim and inculcate the revealed will of God as it bears upon every department of life. (John Murray, "The Church, Its Identity, Function, and Resources" in The Collected Writing of John Murray, vol. 1 (Banner of Truth, 1976), p. 241.)

To the church is committed the task of proclaiming the whole counsel of God and, there, the counsel of God as it bears upon the responsibility of all persons and institutions. While the church is not to discharge the functions of other institutions such as the state and the family, nevertheless it is charged to define what the functions of these institutions are. (John Murray, "The Relation of Church and State," in The Collected Writings of John Murray, vol. 1 (Banner of Truth, 1976, p. 255.)

The struggle to unite body and soul and to join the concern for this world with the concerns of the world to come have been a perpetual issue in Christian thought and practice. Early Church asceticism, Medieval monasticism, Reformation era Anabaptist, Amish and Pietist movements and various modern forms of Christian Fundamentalism are examples of Christian rejections of this worldly concerns for a predominant focus on the world to come. Their criticism have raised authentic concerns about the this-world focus of liberal Protestantism as well as what they view to be the too closely linked varieties of historic Catholicism and Orthodox Communions with the activities of civil governments. The Fundamentalist critique of these Church movements is twofold. The first is that their social/political activism has led to a loss of Gospel proclamation and passionate concern for the eternal destinies of the souls of men. The second is the loss of the personal and corporate godliness called for by Scripture due to the Church's commitment to the rough and tumble politics of partisan agendas.

Various forms of Evangelical and Reformed traditions have sought to affirm legitimacy for the Church to carry out both the Gospel and the social duties that seem to be enjoined by the teachings of Christ. Such texts as Matthew 5:13-15 and John 17:8-19 are considered to be germane for this approach.

Matthew 5:13-16 affirms, "You are the salt of the earth. but if the salt loses its saltiness, how can it be made salty again? It is no longer good for anything, except to be thrown out and trampled by men. You are the light of the world. A city on a hill cannot be hidden. Neither do people light a lamp and put it under a bowl. Instead they put it on its stand, and it gives light to everyone in the house. In the same way, let your light shine before men, that they may see your good deeds and praise your Father in heaven."

John 17:8-14 states, "For I gave them the words you gave me and they accepted them. They knew with certainty that I came from you, and they believed that you sent me. ...I will remain in the world no longer, but they are still in the world, and I am coming to you. Holy Father, protect them by the power of your name--the name you gave me--so that they may be one as we are one. While I was with them, I protected them and kept them safe by the name you gave. . . .I am coming to you now, but I say these things while I am still in the world, so that they may have the full measure of my joy within them. I have given them your word and the world has hated them, for they are not of the world any more than I am of the world. My prayer is not that you take them out of the world but that you protect them from the evil one. They are not of the world even as I am not of it. Sanctify them by the truth; your word is truth. As you sent me into the world, I have sent them into the world. For them I sanctify myself that they too may be truly sanctified."

Thus Christians are in the world but not of the world. They are the salt of the earth and the light of the world. These concepts have led to the view that ultimately there is to be no distinction for the believer between the sacred and the secular. All that the Christian touches is to be influenced by his or her world and thus seeks to impact it, yet all the while doing so by not being of this world.

Finally, Paul explains the idea of a this-worldly impact with an other-worldly methodology in 2 Corinthians 10:3-5, "For though we live in the world, we do not wage war as the world does. The weapons we fight with are not the weapons of the world. On the contrary, they have divine power to demolish strongholds. We demolish arguments and every pretension that sets itself up against the knowledge of God, and we take captive every thought to make it obedient to Christ."

A famous saying attributed to Abraham Kuyper (1836-1920) seems to proclaim this perspective well, "There is not a square inch in the whole domain of our human existence over which Christ, who is Sovereign over all, does not cry: 'Mine!'"

Dr. Peter A. Lillback is Professor of Historical Theology and President of Westminster Theological Seminary in Philadelphia as well as President of The Providence Forum. He is a Teaching Elder in the Presbyterian Church in America (PCA).

From Open Friendship in a Closed Society

"I believe there are more instances of the abridgement of the freedom of the people by gradual and silent encroachments of those in power than by violent and sudden usurpations."

JAMES MADISON

Excerpts From
Open Friendship in a Closed Society

by Peter Slade, Ph.D.

EDITOR'S NOTE: The original publication of the article below contains the names of the individuals and churches involved. It is not our purpose to accuse specific people or groups of wrong-doing; therefore, the work has been edited to remove identifying information, including footnotes. Our purpose in publishing this article is to make readers aware of the inherent danger in the "doctrine" called the *spirituality of the church.*

The concept that "justice is God's job and the laws of our land's job," reiterates a distinctive theological position articulated in a particularly sophisticated form by Southern Presbyterians. Called the *spirituality of the church*, this doctrine was formulated in its most distinct and influential form in the nineteenth century by Southern Presbyterians to defend the privileged and powerful from the intrusion of abolitionist morality into their religion. It became a trust doctrinal bulwark against the continued intrusion of carpetbaggers, scallywags, liberals, ecumenists, and civil rights activists into the Southern way of life.

In the summer of 1954, one prominent Southern Presbyterian church stood with its state legislature and the newly organized Citizens' Councils in their determination to challenge the federal ruling (Supreme Court, *Brown vs. Board of Education of Topeka, Kansas*) and defend white supremacy. This church distinguished itself by having one of two church sessions in the PCUS that *unanimously* dissented from the denomination's support of *Brown vs. Board*. Its elders issued a statement denouncing the Assembly's recommendation as wrong to claim that segregation of the races was discrimination. Such a suggestion threatened "the peace and purity of the church"; consequently, this particular church would "maintain its traditional practice of distinct separation of the races." The church received the support of the state Synod, which sent an overture to the next General Assembly asking them to rescind the statement and "to redefine the functions of the ...Council on Christian Relations."

No matter how erudite the arguments for segregation, and there were many, the strongest case against the Presbyterian church's denunciation of segregation still rested not in theological cases for segregation but in an appeal to the spirituality of the church. In 1957, in a carefully worded response to further pronouncements by the Council on Christian Relations, the church in question set out its case against the church's interference in the political issue of segregation:

> The Session does not feel that the Presbyterian Church in
> the United States should take any action with reference
> to current social, political and economic problems...
> an organized church should exist only for the purpose
> of stimulating and strengthening its members and for
> coordinating and implementing their activities in bringing
> others to know Him and serve Him.

The individual Christian should "seek to correct injustices and defects in our social, political and economic order" but exactly what constitutes an injustice should remain a "private judgment in all secular matters." Published in the pages of *The Southern Presbyterian Journal*, the statement objected to the General Assembly's condemnation of severe literacy tests as requirements for voting, segregated schools, and the Citizens' Councils. It also strongly contested the notion that "freedom of fellowship" should extend to "an unnatural association of people."

Members of the church, who included some of the most powerful and influential men in the city, tended to use their "private judgment in all secular matters" to defend the existing social, political, and economic order. The church itself encouraged its members in their participation in the Citizens' Councils: in the 1957 statement the Session declared, "There are numerous citizen's councils and groups throughout the South which are composed of Christian citizens of the highest type." Elders of the church were involved at the highest level in the Citizens' Council. Two attorneys and highly regarded elders in the church served as directors of the city's Citizens' Council. Civil rights activists were well aware of the church's support for the organization Hodding Carter called the "Uptown Klan" and labeled its minister "chaplain of the white Citizens' Council of the State."

One elder/lawyer, in his professional capacity as attorney for the city, had a grandstand view of the changes that activists backed by federal legislation were trying to bring to the state; he defended the city when the NAACP brought a case against the city's segregated public schools. Another elder, a circuit court judge, signed off on an order allowing police to send civil rights activists straight to prison, and also presided over a farcical trial in which a white defendant was accused of murdering a black man; the all-white jury was unable to reach a verdict and the white defendant walked free. [The defendant was later convicted.]

In 1963, the pastor of the church received word from a Methodist minister in Connecticut that he would be visiting the church with a group of black and white students currently attending a World Council of Churches' work camp nearby. While policemen hovered nearby in case of trouble, ushers barred nine white and two black students from entering the church. The Citizen's Council shared the church's resolve to "maintain its traditional practice of distinct separation of the races." In late September, with two of the church's elders serving as directors, the press reported that the Citizen's Council "would develop a plan to eliminate integration in local churches."

Peter Slade teaches courses in the History of Christianity and Christian Thought at Ashland University in Ohio. He received his doctorate degree in

Religious Studies from the University of Virginia. Prior to studying at UVa, Slade earned an M.A. in Southern Studies from the University of Mississippi and a B.D.with Honors in Christian Ethics and Practical Theology from St. Andrews University, Scotland.

Permission granted from Oxford University Press to use the following quotes from Open Friendship in a Closed Society: Mission Mississippi and a Theology of Friendship by Peter Slade, 20009: pp. 94, 107-110

Fighting the Gay-Marriage Goliath

What's the Role of Pastors?

"The wrath of God is being revealed from heaven against all the godlessness and wickedness of men who suppress the truth by their wickedness, since what may be known about God is plain to them, because God made it plain to them."

ROMANS 1:18, 19

Fighting the Gay-Marriage Goliath
What's the Role of Pastors?

by Paul Kengor

As Americans arrogate unto themselves the right to redefine the laws of nature and nature's God, faithful Christians stare in amazement at their culture's willingness to fundamentally transform the multi-millennia standard of male-female marriage. What has caused this rapid shift? The answers are varied, of course, but what's clear is that the church has lost to the more dominant forces of Hollywood, social media, relativism, individualism, progressivism, and the rest of the growing cultural-secular miasma that now shapes this nation's values.

And so, how should the church respond? Can pastors navigate the way out of this mess, rather than the government dictating the terms of something as rudimentary as the standards of marriage and family? Morally and ethically, can Reformed leaders *lead*. Are they willing to take action?

The answer is they have no other choice; if they don't come for the culture, the culture will come for them. Pastors and churches MUST lead. Really, only Christian churches, being Christian, can even get away with the argument that gay "marriage" is not actually marriage. It's more difficult for a politician to successfully advance that argument in the public square, but the argument is absolutely within the purview and authority of churches.

As a case in point, I'd like to rattle the sensibilities and raise the eyebrows of this readership, which is, obviously, mostly Protestant and particularly PCA-based, with an example it isn't expecting here. I'd like to share the quite instructive example of the Roman Catholic Church on the marriage/family issue from the mid-1800s into the 21st century. I've laid this out in one of the chapters of my new book, _Takedown: From Communists to Progressives, How the Left Has Sabotaged Family and Marriage_. I've long been aware of the Catholic Church's longtime fight against communism and the radical-secular left, but not until I dug deeper did I see how it specifically countered the far left's ongoing attempts to redefine marriage and family. It's a story of remarkable institutional consistency, with lessons for all faithful Christians still standing for natural-traditional-biblical marriage, including PCA pastors who need to step up.

Beginning in the 1800s, rabidly atheistic leftists, from socialist utopians like Robert Owen and Charles Fourier to communists like Karl Marx and Friedrich Engels, sought to tear down religion and traditional family and marriage. Marx and Engels in the _Communist Manifesto_ in 1848 wrote openly of "the abolition of the family," which, even then, they could refer to as "an infamous proposal of the Communists."

It was infamous enough that in Rome two years earlier, Pope Pius IX began his long pontificate with the encyclical _Qui pluribus_ (On Faith and Religion), released in November 1846. The first of many Pius IX statements, it eviscerated "the unspeakable doctrine of Communism, as it is called, a doctrine most opposed to the very natural law." Pius IX predicted severe destruction, including moral damage, and specifically warned that communism would violate "the sanctity of marriage."

Pius IX was succeeded by another long-serving pope, Leo XIII. Likewise in the first year of his pontificate, this pontiff zeroed in on the secular left's moral wreckage. On April 21, 1878, he released his first encyclical, _Inscrutabili Dei Consilio_ (On the Evils of Society), and then three days after Christmas released the second, _Quod Apostolici muneris_ (On Socialism).

In _Quod Apostolici muneris_, Pope Leo XIII identified the evils that had "so rapidly increased" in such a short term—reminiscent of our own day.

They were being perpetrated by "socialists, communists, nihilists" and others who "openly and boldly marching forth in the light of day, strive to bring to a head what they have long been planning—the overthrow of all civil society whatsoever." They were looking to transform the most basic elements of society. "They leave nothing untouched or whole which by both human and divine laws has been wisely decreed for the health and beauty of life," stated the encyclical. "They refuse obedience to the higher powers, to whom, according to the admonition of the Apostle, every soul ought to be subject, and who derive the right of governing from God."

Among the beauties of life they foul up, said Leo XIII, is marriage and the family: "They debase the natural union of man and woman, which is held sacred even among barbarous peoples; and its bond, by which the family is chiefly held together, they weaken, or even deliver up to lust." They attack "even family life itself, which is the cornerstone of all society and government." The encyclical stated that the foundation of society "rests first of all in the indissoluble union of man and wife according to the necessity of natural law, and is completed in the mutual rights and duties of parents and children, masters and servants." And yet, "the doctrines of socialism strive almost completely to dissolve this union." Leo XIII added that, "The Church, on the contrary, teaches that 'marriage, honorable in all,' which God himself instituted in the very beginning of the world, and made indissoluble for the propagation and preservation of the human species."

The extreme left, these socialists and communists and nihilists spread throughout the world and bound in a "wicked confederacy" against God's design for man, threatened these precious things.

After Leo XIII, a succession of popes echoed these warnings in major pronouncements in 1924, 1928, 1930, 1931, 1932 (two statements that year), 1933, and with the harshest still yet to come: In March 1937, Pope Pius XI issued the Church's most scathing attack on ascendant communist ideology, which it called a "satanic scourge," and took specific aim at communism's attack on marriage and family. Pius XI instructed the flock that holy "matrimony" is of "divine origin," and was "fundamental" and "fixed" by the Creator.

This consistency in defending marriage continues in Rome today, without references to communism but instead to radical individualism, to what Pope Francis has called "adolescent progressivism," and to what Pope Benedict XVI and Pope Francis both have called the "dictatorship of relativism." Despite Pope Francis' leftward leanings on certain issues, he and his bishops (especially the American bishops) have not flinched in upholding their faith's core teachings on family and marriage. In January, Francis explicitly warned against "forms of ideological colonization which are out to destroy the family" and that seek to "redefine the very institution of marriage, by relativism." He has asserted that marriage must remain between one man and one woman—who bring an essential, natural, and divinely ordained male-female "complementarity" to parenting—and that every child has a "right" to a mother and a father. He has stated that same-sex parenting "discriminates against the child in advance," depriving the child of a natural right to a mom and dad. And yet, Francis has also famously reached out to homosexuals in strikingly understanding, sympathetic, and merciful language—so much so that countless liberals actually mistakenly think this pope supports gay marriage, a remarkably ignorant misinterpretation of his tone (which they find appealing) rather than his teaching. He has loved the sinners but not their sins, nor their insistence that loving them means accepting their redefinition of marriage.

There is, in short, a lesson here for Reformed pastors and churches and, really, pastors and churches of all stripes. From Pope Francis today back to the likes of Pope Pius IX two centuries ago, there has been a striking moral and institutional consistency from Rome on marriage, with the only adaptation being not core teaching but a merciful tone that preaches and reaches. Will it work in repelling the gay-marriage Goliath in modern American and Western culture? Maybe, maybe not. Nonetheless, it MUST be tried. There is no other option.

Reformed pastors in churches like PCA, while obviously disagreeing with the Rome on certain notable doctrines, should take heed of these leadership lessons on family and marriage. Ironically, when it comes to family and marriage, evangelical pastors can take better example from Rome than they can from the PCUSA general assembly.

Dr. Paul Kengor is professor of political science at Grove City College. His latest book is Takedown: From Communists to Progressives, How the Left Has Sabotaged Family and Marriage. He has written over a dozen books, including 11 Principles of a Reagan Conservative.

The Christian
and Civil Disobedience

"While we must always be subject to the office of the magistrate, we are not to be subject to the man in that office who commands that which is contrary to the Bible."

FRANCIS SCHAEFFER

The Christian
and Civil Disobedience

by Jerry Newcombe

R ecent events have called into question the issue of obeying the government in all ways--even in all circumstances.

In the 13th chapter of Romans, Paul says that God has given us the government as a minister of righteousness. It is our duty to obey it. But we also see in Scripture that on occasion, when the government calls for one to disobey God, then civil disobedience is in order.

There's a great lesson to learn from one aspect of World War II related to distortions of Romans 13. I'm not calling anybody a Nazi, but consider this lengthy lesson, wherein the Nazis quoted Scripture in order to demand unquestioning obedience.

On April 9, 1940, without any warning or provocation, the Germans invaded Norway. It was an unexpected battle and an unfair fight with 400,000 German Wehrmacht versus a nation not expecting it. This nightmare lasted until May 1945.

There were, of course, Norwegian collaborators--Norwegians who sold their soul to get ahead during the reign of the Nazis. Foremost amongst them was Vidkun Quisling. His name has been adopted into the dictionary: A quisling is a traitor.

When the Nazis took over Norway, a country full of "pure Aryans," they expected the Norwegians to fully participate in their attempts to glorify the "master race" and purge the "undesirables" from humanity, such as Jews, Gypsies, and Slavs.

The Norwegians would have nothing to do with this. So they resisted, usually in every peaceful way they could. Much of the battle was fought over distributing accurate information.

In Oslo, there is a museum (Norges Hjemmefront Museum) dedicated to the resistance movement in World War II. They have a plaque there in English: "In Norway, Nazi ideology was defeated by the democratic forces rooted in a national, Christian culture."

While the Nazis won militarily (until the end of the war), they never came close to winning the hearts and minds of the people.

Normally, in those days, the churches were full. But during the war, something happened to cause the churches to go empty. The Norwegian bishops and priests, desiring to be faithful to God and the Scriptures, resisted the Nazi efforts to control the churches and the content of sermons. The clergy reasoned that if they all resisted together as one, nothing could happen to them. They were all arrested and sent to concentration camps. Most of them never returned.

Many Norwegian Christians met in private homes secretly for worship and avoided the churches during the war.

The same thing happened with the school teachers. The Nazis took over the curriculum of the schools. The teachers resisted as one group. They too were arrested and sent to concentration camps. Most never returned.

The museum contains a 1941 book, written in Norwegian used in the schools by the Nazis. In it, they quote Scripture: "What are those called in Romans 13:1 who God has set over us? Have you considered that your parents, your school teachers (your principal), policemen, police chief, judges, the priest, the bishop, the county commission, the state government, are the authorities who are installed by God, and that you owe them obedience?"

Then it says: "Overall, we owe the Fuhrer and the government obedience. If you set yourself up against the authorities and against the state, you are standing against God's structure and are subject to punishment."

Talk about the devil quoting Scripture. In reality, the Fuhrer was hostile toward Christianity. Hitler once declared, "The heaviest blow that ever struck humanity was the coming of Christianity. Bolshevism is Christianity's illegitimate child. Both are inventions of the Jew." But he was happy to have his minions twist the Christian Scriptures for his own ends.

God's Word is pure and right. But that doesn't mean it can't be distorted sometimes by evil people intent on achieving goals that are contrary to the message of Scripture. There's a time and a place for everything under the sun, including (on occasion) civil disobedience.

Recently I came across an unpublished letter by D. James Kennedy (11/29/1988), in which he addressed this issue: "The basic Bible principles, I believe, are these: 1) All authority is from God. 2) All human authority is delegated from God. 3) No human authority can countermand the authority of God. 4) If such anti-biblical laws are passed, Christians must in conscience disobey them. 5) They must be prepared to suffer the consequences of their actions."

Then he solidifies the whole point: "The very existence of Christianity depends upon Christians obeying these principles. Had they not done so, Christianity, which was outlawed first in Israel and then in the Roman Empire, would have ceased to exist many centuries ago."

Jerry Newcombe is senior TV producer / on-air personality of Kennedy Classics. He has written/co-written 25 books, including The Book That Made America, Doubting Thomas *(w/ Mark Beliles, on Jefferson),* What If Jesus Had Never Been Born? *(w/ D. James Kennedy) &* George Washington's Sacred Fire *(w/ Peter Lillback)*

The Reality of Jesus
in Africa

"Faith in Action – God in Motion"

AFRICAN BIBLE COLLEGE MOTTO

The Reality of Jesus in Africa

by Nell Robertson Chinchen

I Met Him Under Very Unusual Circumstances

A ctually, I thought I knew Him...After all, didn't I always go to Sunday School and Church? Didn't I recite the Shorter Catechism? Didn't I say "now I lay me down to sleep" every night? I believed. I believed everything I was told about God. I certainly didn't want to go to hell! And I believed there was a hell for all the bad people. I certainly didn't want to be one of THOSE!

SO, it really came as sort of a shock when my eight-month-old baby daughter came down with pneumonia and ended up in the hospital. Suddenly, I realized I could not pray with any assurance that God would listen to my prayers. I frantically called my brother, Palmer Robertson, whom I knew had direct access to that Throne of Grace. Somehow, that experience opened up my heart to desire to get closer to the One who died on that cross.

Soon after that, Palmer came to work in our orchards. He stepped off the train with...of all things...a Bible in his hands. It was a little embarrassing for me. This was California. Not the "Bible Belt"! I was no longer a "true southerner." I now belonged to an entirely different culture. NO ONE... absolutely NO ONE...in our crowd or even in my husband Jack's religious Methodist family carried a Bible around in public. In fact, there was not even one in Jack's parents' or grandparent's home. Jack himself had never even owned a Bible. But of course, he and his family were Christians. Methodist, that is.

We watched in amazement as this teen-age boy would get up early in the morning before going to work in the pear orchards to read his Bible. We were surprised to find there were churches open on Wednesday and Sunday nights. This was the "heathen wild west" as my Mother called it. And yet, Palmer managed to find one and off he would go, leaving us somewhat convicted and yet not understanding why.

One day my curiosity overwhelmed my Christian ethics and while he was at work, I went quietly into his bedroom and STOLE his Bible. It was a recent transliteration and very easy to read and understand. As I continued to read, I came to such passages as "What does it profit a man if he gains the whole world and loses his soul?" Soon, I came to a decision: "If these things are true. I had better DO SOMETHING ABOUT IT?" The phrase that I made a conscious decision on was "I'M GOING TO PUT ALL MY EGGS IN ONE BASKET,' in other words, count on it being true!

From then on, I wanted more. Before Palmer left that summer, he gave me a book for my birthday, *My Burden Is Light* by Eugenia Price. This is when I met Jesus the Christ. This is when I realized He was a real person. I knew He was real because I found myself being very jealous of the way Eugenia Price referred to Him. I hated her. She talked like she was in love with Him. She can't do that! He's mine! I was very, very jealous. I didn't like her at all. I thought she was brazen to talk about Him like that.

I was really in love. All the symptoms were there. I spent hours on my knees talking to Him--mostly crying and pleading for my husband to become not only a Christian but to yield to the pressure of the Holy Spirit to go into Christian service...to become a missionary so I could fully dedicate my life to the one with whom I had fallen in love.

And it did happen. Prayers were answered and He became as real to Jack as He was to me. Jack wept when he read of His crucifixion. He listened when God called him to walk away from all our possessions and family and take his little family off to seminary. He listened when God called us to a remote mission church in Washington state, and he listened when my prayers were finally answered and God called us to the jungles in Africa.

The Reality of Jesus is Very Evident in Africa

It has to be. Satanic powers are so strong, having been strengthened for thousands of years by having no restrictions from the Holy Spirit. The Holy Spirit indwells human beings. He is not an invisible cloud. Missionaries, filled with the Holy Spirit, tried time and time again to penetrate the darkness of those jungles in Liberia, West Africa, to no avail. There were too many obstacles. Disease, death, isolation all were like chains holding back the Gospel. The witchcraft, the ju ju worship, the superstitions were strong bands that were almost impossible to break.

We felt helpless as time after time we battled these deep rooted obstacles to bring the reality of Jesus to those blinded by the powers of darkness. When the "devil dancer" first came to our house and everyone ran for cover, even I felt the fear that hung in the air. When his helper asked for money, I gave him 30 cents. I was desperate to move this evil being from my house and I knew all the people on the mission station were trembling with terror. Later, when my husband said, "Why did you give money to the devil?" I was so convicted of my sin, I suffered the pangs of repentance. I had forgotten that "He that is in you is stronger than he that is in the world". I had lost the reality of Christ in a moment of fear.

Fear is Satan's most powerful weapon in Africa. It is engrained even in the youngest child. Babies quickly have a string tied around their waist to ward off the evil spirits. "Ju jus" around the neck offer protection from the attacks of Satan. He reigns supreme. Multitudes and multitudes of superstitions cannot be overcome even by the preaching of the Gospel. It is easy for the African to accept Christ, but not easy to supplant those mysterious beliefs that have captivated them for thousands of years.

Our daughter, Lisa, was asked to visit a remote village by one of our faithful workers. It was several hours walk through the jungle so we sent her older brother with her. They gave her a room in their mud hut, but she said as she lay down on the little bed and looked up , there hanging from the ceiling was the ugliest face she had ever seen. It was carved out of wood but had the appearance of being real. The next morning she asked the worker, Moses, what it was. He answered in all seriousness, "Lisa, that's my father's Ju Ju. Every day he brings it rice and water. Lisa, pray for my father." Certainly, Moses, as a Christian, had tried to teach his father to forsake his idols, but his father was old and the tradition too deeply rooted for him to give up for someone he did not know was actually a real person. His fear of Satan was too strong.

The presence of Christ on the mission field has to be real enough to impart the courage needed to be protected from the wiles of the devil. His tactics are not new and yet they always seem to come unexpectedly.

Sickness stalks those jungle trails as well as busier metropolitan cities. For centuries, the mosquito has carried out the job of keeping missionaries out of Africa. Yellow fever and malaria have yet to be conquered. Lassa fever and more recently, the ebola virus have discouraged those who long to take the Gospel and seek to open blinded eyes. It is just one more obstacle thrown out by Satan to hinder the reality of Christ from bringing freedom to those in bondage.

More recently, Islamic radicalism has crept into the void left by departing missionaries and national Christians seeking to escape the snares of the satanic practices. Africans easily fall prey to this perverted religion with its promises and pledges of a better life. Young children are early on indoctrinated to the cruelty and abuse the Muslims use to instill fear. Their tactics are designed to force loyalty to their religion on young and old alike. Even over 20 years ago, pastors in the northern region of Liberia were boiled in oil for refusing to accept the Muslim faith. Fear is always the tool that Satan uses to make converts and the Islamic religion is no exception.

Discouragement goes hand in hand with that fear. Loss of courage indicates a loss of faith. When the darkness of night envelopes the darkness of the jungle, it is difficult to hold on to the belief that the promises God has made are actually true. That the One who wrote them is a very real person. This is why it is so vital that the reality of Christ somehow be imparted to the African. That can only be done as He is seen in us. It is imperative that we manifest this One who is so alive and lives within us.

When we arrived as new missionaries to the small, somewhat insignificant country of Liberia, West Africa, we were flown in a little Cessna 180 to a remote mission station harbored in the thickest forests of all Africa. The plane set down between those trees on a 750 foot airstrip. As we looked out the window we could see the native people had built us a bamboo house up on stilts. We lived in that house without water or electricity for two years. But one day, that little house we had come to love caught fire and burned to the ground. As we stood on the airstrip and watched as flames consumed all our earthly possessions, we could hear the wailing of all the people surrounding us. They had come even from the nearby villages to watch this alarming demonstration of Satan's attempt to discourage not only us, but all the people we were there to serve as well. One of the small children took off her sandals and quietly slipped them on our daughter Marion's feet. She was barely 4 years old but they all knew our children were not to be barefooted on that parasite infected ground. As we walked away from the heartbreaking sight, our fourteen-year-old daughter, Lisa, turned to me and said, "Mother, remember what the Bible says, 'Lay not up for yourselves treasures on earth, but lay up for yourselves treasures in heaven where neither moth nor rust does corrupt..or fire consume!..but lay up for yourselves treasures in heaven…"

I needed that reminder, and I knew it was true. It became apparent later when one of the pastors in training came to us and said he wanted to talk to our whole family. We gathered the children about us and listened carefully as he began speaking. "My people sent me to say thank you."
I said, "For what?"

He answered, "For what you have taught us. When your house burned down, and you lost everything you had brought into this jungle, you did not cry and wail as we did. You were smiling. You showed us that all those things you had did not mean as much to you as the Jesus you have been telling us about."

We did not know they were watching us. I do know that in that time of testing, Jesus was very real. And He was using that trial to demonstrate to these people, His reality.

We also witnessed the reality of His healing power. We had not been in the jungles of Liberia long when one day the nearby village people came in a small group to our little bamboo house and begged me to come with them to see a little girl who had fallen into the fire. I quickly grabbed my jar of Furacin ointment and some bandages, along with soap and boiled water. Nevertheless, I was not prepared for what I saw. The girl was only about 8 years old. Her name was Comfort. She had evidently fallen into the fire and burned her face and neck until they were like charcoal. Not only was her face swollen but her eyes were completely swollen shut. She was lying on bamboo slats in the dark mud hut. I told the people, "Please bring her outside so I can see her better." They set up a woven mat chair outside and when I looked at her face, it was easy to see they had already applied their "country Medicine" of dirt, leaves and cow manure. Then I was told the accident had happened two days earlier. Infection had already set in.

As the people hovered over the chair, I said, "Please tell her I am going to have to scrub her face and it will hurt. Someone will need to hold her." Comfort answered back in her dialect, "They do not need to hold me. I will not fight." And she didn't. But I knew if I left her there in the village, they would once again apply their country medicine, and she could easily die from the infection. So I asked them to let me take her home with me where I could dress that horrible burn every day and give her the penicillin shots she needed to overcome this infected burn.

Comfort quickly adapted to our household. She loved the little jars of meat sticks I had brought from the states for our baby Marion; she wanted me to sing to her every night, "For God So Loved the World" Even though she did not really understand English, she seemed to capture the meaning of that song about salvation. Soon, we were able to communicate with her and it wasn't long before she received Jesus as her Savior. He had become real to her. And not only that, but another miracle took place--her face healed without a scar. Even secular doctors have called it a miracle when they see the pictures of Comfort's face.

The simple belief of a child, however, is soon overshadowed by what we call Statism. As society becomes more and more sophisticated, this ideology supplants God as the One who is All-Powerful. R.C. Sproul writes: "Statism happens when the government is perceived as or claims to be the ultimate reality. This reality then replaces God as the supreme entity upon which human existence depends."

Time after time what we have seen in Africa is an all-powerful God performing miracles. The day of miracles has not passed. But what has happened is that an all-powerful God has been supplanted by a so-called all-powerful government. This is Statism. Not only does this ideology affect our own nation but it extends its greedy hands across the ocean and seeks to control the rest of the world. Even Africa.

With no qualms whatsoever, the government of our country sought to destroy an innocent little country called Liberia where my husband and I serve as missionaries. Liberia's motto is "The love of liberty brought us here." Settled by freed American slaves in 1820, Liberia had been a peaceful democracy for 150 years. One day I had a visitor, a representative from the United States Embassy, who had driven over 200 miles to call on me and other Americans in Nimba County. This type of call was being made all across Liberia.

She began our conversation with a statement followed by a question: "We at the United States Embassy feel it's time for a change. It is time for the native Liberians to have rule over Liberia. What do you think?"

I answered in shock, "I can't believe you said that. I would like you to repeat it to my husband so I understand what you are saying." Jack's reaction was the same as mine…Liberia had been a peaceful nation for 150 years. Why change?

That was the beginning of the end. Shortly after that visit, there was a coup d'etat. In April of 1980 President William Tolbert, our Christian president, was brutally murdered in his bed by a few soldiers led by Samuel K. Doe, from the Krahn tribe in southern Liberia, and this soldier with an eighth grade education was now the president of the Republic of Liberia. The outcome of the Coup d'etat did not live up to the expectations of the US Embassy. So, another plan materialized.

On November 12, 1985, a man by the name of Thomas Quiwonkpa, from the Mano-Gio tribe, attempted another coup. We had been warned by the Military Attache to the US Embassy that a "bloodless coup" was about to take place. Missionaries at the ELWA Mission Station in Monrovia were advised by the US Embassy to stay in their homes on the day of the anticipated invasion of General Quiwonkpa and his men.

It all happened very quickly and as planned. Quiwonkpa captured President Samuel K Doe and then announced over the ELWA radio station that he was now the President of Liberia. There was much rejoicing and dancing in the streets, even in Yekepa, 200 miles away, where the African Bible College is located. But suddenly everything changed. Sergeant Doe bribed his way out of captivity. The tide turned drastically. Quiwonkpa was mercilessly killed, the ELWA Mission, because General Thomas Quiwonkpa had broadcast over their radio station his claim to be the new president, was hit by rockets carried on a vehicle called the "Russian Organ" and fired from Sophie's Ice Cream Parlor. The ELWA Radio Station, whose signals reached all across the African Continent was now completely destroyed.

But the big, all-powerful government of the USA had promised to help! Quiwonkpa was not to do this overthrow alone! He had been promised the all-powerful one was to be standing by ….standing with him in this venture.

This entire episode is graphically documented, along with the ensuing genocide of the Mano/Gio Tribes, in the book Liberia: *A Promise Betrayed* by Bill Berkeley (Lawyers for Human Rights Committee, 1986).

Statists are like hungry lions walking about "seeking someone to devour" (1 Peter 5:8) and conquer. Their lust for more power is never satisfied; thus, the desire for our "big government" to reach beyond our own borders and control the world. Liberia has been an easy target. This is why the belief in an all-powerful God is so necessary to prevent this deception.

II Chronicles 7:14 promises, "If my people who are called by my Name will humble themselves and pray and seek my face and turn from their wicked ways, then will I hear from heaven and will forgive their sin and will heal their land."

There is "healing in His wings". Our God is powerful enough to rule the world. We need to look beyond the empty promises made by the politicians, to look beyond the powers of government, and trust in the living and true God who alone can bring back the righteousness to our nation…yea, to the world that has been lost.

The reality of Jesus must become real to the whole world if Statism is to be defeated. Even as He appeared as an angel to Lot (what the theologians call a theophany) and urged him to flee the wrath of God which was to come, even so we, who have encountered the living Christ, must proclaim Him to a world which has been blinded by unbelief.

Charlie Rodriguez, publisher, wrote this to me when God, in answer to multitudes of prayers, performed a miracle of healing on me:

"The secular world and its governing authorities don't believe in miracles. Although unbelievers here and in Africa have different ways of explaining your miraculous healing, it all amounts to the same thing—an unbelief in an all powerful and loving God who delights in performing miracles so that many might believe in Him rather than in the government.."

Certainly, I can affirm, not only from what I have seen and heard, but from my own personal experience in the miracle of God's healing power, that the reality of the Christ exists….even in Africa.

Nell Robertson Chinchen is a missionary to Africa and co-founder of African Bible Colleges, with campuses in Liberia, Malawi, and Uganda.

A Spiritual Church
is Society's Best Friend

"Christianity is not just involved with "salvation", but with the total man in the total world. The Christian message begins with the existence of God forever, and then with creation. It does not begin with salvation. We must be thankful for salvation, but the Christian message is more than that. Man has a value because he is made in the image of God."

FRANCIS A. SCHAEFFER, *ART & THE BIBLE*

A Spiritual Church is Society's Best Friend

by Aaron Menikoff

We've all heard the phrase, "He's so heavenly-minded he's no earthly good." It conveys the image of a Christian meditating on Scripture, eyes closed and seemingly lost in some kind of tranquil bliss. Meanwhile, the world crumbles around him—children are made sex-slaves, babies are aborted, teenagers are in foster care, Klan knights are marching down Main Street, Christians are beheaded in the Middle East, and religious liberty is ignored at home. What good is a faith that won't confront these challenges? What good is a faith that does no good?

Too often inaction has marked God's people. We look no further than nineteenth-century America, when evangelical Christians did more than tolerate slavery; they approved and promoted it. We look no further than Nazi Germany, when the church cowered under the proclamations of a madman. My own grandfather, a boy from what is now Belarus, found himself the victim of a pogrom. He hung on a tree with a Communist rope tied around his Jewish neck until his father cut him down. We look no further than a Birmingham jail, when Martin Luther King Jr. had to defend his campaign of nonviolent resistance to, of all people, pastors.

The Gospel A Catalyst to Action

In response to such inaction, some churches have neglected or even abandoned the gospel. They wave the banner of social justice, argue that doctrine divides, and accuse the "heavenly-minded" of cutting James 1:27 out of the Bible. Best-selling author Jim Wallis wrote in *The Uncommon Good* that the gospel of Jesus Christ is secondary to social change. Creedal convictions, Wallis insists, are less important than social commitments. Since preaching the gospel takes a backseat to doing good, Wallis argues it doesn't matter if one is Christian, Jewish, or Muslim so long as one responds to injustice in the world.

Wallis's view ignores the heart of Christianity and the words of its founder. As Jesus said, "For what does it profit a man to gain the whole world and forfeit his life?" (Mark 8:36) This Jewish carpenter had an extraordinary interest in the souls of men and women made in God's image. Without neglecting the body (he healed numerous invalids and fed thousands), Jesus emphasized getting spiritually right with a sovereign God: "Do not fear those who kill the body but cannot kill the soul. Rather fear him who can destroy both soul and body in hell" (Matthew 10:28). Jesus taught a church without the gospel is like a well without water; it may look refreshing from a distance but has nothing life-giving to offer the parched.

In light of Jesus' teaching, what the world needs is not less gospel preaching, but more. The world needs not less heavenly-mindedness, but a better vision of the new heavens and new earth. The world needs not less spiritual churches, but more churches devoted to the faithful exposition of God's Word. A spiritual church is best equipped to give the world what it desperately needs: the message of everlasting life. And this gospel of grace will, by design, speak against the injustice and inhumanity that feed the moral wreckage of the twenty-first century. God does not guarantee peace and prosperity in the here-and-now, but his gospel of grace promotes the virtues that every society needs to flourish.

Over fifty years ago Francis Schaeffer noted how America adopted "an almost monolithic consensus" against traditional morality. Virtue, Schaeffer argued, no longer serves as a bedrock principle of the good life. Instead of individuals protecting universal truths that benefit society, society defends interpretations of reality that benefit individuals. Admittedly, some of these personal interpretations promote social well-being. For example, many irreligious persons fight poverty and protect the environment. But such do-gooders pick and choose which personal interpretations of reality to impose on others. While guarding the Everglades they cringe at the thought of defunding Planned Parenthood lest a woman's right to choose plays second fiddle to a baby's right to live. Such cherry picking of virtue is not virtue at all; it is self-interest masked as morality. In light of such changes, Schaeffer famously asked, "How shall we then live?"

Christians have failed to live up to the precepts of their faith. We should respond with remorse and repentance. We must avoid the sins of our evangelical predecessors who failed to speak up when social sins reared their ugly head. However we must be just as disciplined to hold tightly to the gospel. It doesn't ultimately matter if a church has a social conscience if it has lost its gospel heart. Thankfully, we don't have to pit gospel ministry against social concern. A church committed to sound doctrine will be full of Christians eager to be of social good.

Society's fundamental problem is not a Christianity that has become overly spiritual, but one that isn't spiritual enough. A truly "spiritual" faith is marked by a robust commitment to God's Word, the Bible. As the Bible is taught and obeyed, Christians will lean into the culture instead of leaning away. They engage the culture instead of burying their heads in the sand. They bring the gospel of God's glorious grace to bear on the besetting sins of a fallen world. They preach the virtues of the creator God that the world needs in order to prosper. They live with the prophetic compassion that marked our Lord Jesus Christ himself. And they are not satisfied with an earth that has been morally renovated; they work to see a world redeemed. In that sense, a spiritual church really is society's best friend.

Of course the Christian engages the culture with no divine guarantee the culture will improve. In other words, the church shouldn't promise to put an end to poverty. Jesus wasn't being pessimistic when he said we'd always have the poor with us (Matthew 26:11). He simply taught that suffering persists in a fallen world. Jesus wanted us to understand our hope cannot be in this world. We are to long for the new heavens and new earth. We labor for the common good because it's right, not because we know we will make a difference. We preach because it's truth, not because we know it will be believed. We live in light of the gospel of God's grace because that's the loving thing to do, not because we can be sure others will see it that way as well.

The Prophetic Compassion of Booth & Barrow

Two pastors of a previous generation, both from my tradition, serve as models of evangelical social engagement. They are examples not because they were successful, but because they were
faithful. By applying the Bible to the problems of the day, in the face of great opposition, they lived with a prophetic compassion worthy of contemporary examination.

Starting in 1769 and for the last thirty-seven years of his life, Abraham Booth served as pastor of Little Prescot Church in Goodman's Field, London. Booth's book, *The Reign of Grace*, published in 1768, had caught the attention of the church's leaders who went to hear this country preacher. In *Reign of Grace* he presented a warm Calvinism that promotes both evangelism and practical holiness. This is exactly what the church wanted and needed to hear. Duly impressed by Booth's wisdom and zeal, they persuaded him to leave Nottinghamshire for an urban post.

Twenty years later, Booth preached a sermon from the Little Prescot pulpit that distinguished him as a preacher of prophetic compassion. In *Commerce in the Human Species, and the Enslaving of Innocent Persons, Inimical to the Laws of Moses and the Gospel of Christ*, Booth spoke against the trading of African slaves. The Atlantic slave trade had become a boon to the British economy and spread slavery throughout the New World. The decade prior to his sermon, the Atlantic slave trade reached its peak with 325,500 slaves exported from Africa between 1781 and 1790. By preaching against it, Booth offended much of London's merchant class.

54

Booth based his message on Exodus 21:16, "He that stealeth a man and selleth him, or if he be found in his hand, he shall surely be put to death." The trade in Africans was a sin prohibited not only by Moses in Exodus 21 but by Paul in 1 Timothy 1. God unequivocally and universally condemns such action. Therefore, Booth preached against the slave trade. He also encouraged his church to pray for its demise and to give financially toward benevolent societies committed to the same cause.

Booth did not preach on politics lightly. He knew the pulpit exists to spread the gospel of God's grace. Before he would preach on such a topic, Booth determined the message had to pass a three-pronged test. The message had to be "consistent with the commands of divine law, the grace of the glorious gospel, and the solemnization of public worship." In other words, the truth of the Bible, the gospel, and church had to be at stake. Booth saw each threatened by a society committed to trading in human flesh. How could he read his Bible and ignore the prohibition against man-stealing? How could he preach the gospel and neglect the reality that in Christ there is neither black nor white? How could he gather a church to sing and pray and hear God's Word while ignoring the moral injustice many of his own brothers and sisters condoned? He could not, and so he spoke.

Booth's Christian ministry contributed toward the end of the British slave trade. He saw slavery itself as an attack on "the principles of Christianity." Sadly, Booth did not get to see the fruit of his labors. Britain outlawed the "commerce in human species" a year after his death. Nonetheless, Booth's preaching laid the groundwork for a prophetic compassion worthy of the name, evangelical.

David Barrow, a contemporary of Booth, argued for the end of slavery in the newly formed United States of America. In his twenties Barrow proudly fought on the side of the Patriots during the Revolutionary War. He eventually joined the ministry, moved West, and by 1805 had become a seasoned Kentucky pastor. Barrow had no patience for the spreading rot of slavery.

Slavery offended God's justice and corroded the integrity of the nation. Barrow preached against it because he loved his neighbors, black and white, and feared for the soul of a nation that ran roughshod over a people based simply on the color of their skin. He published his thoughts in 1808. Throughout the jeremiad is Barrow's desire for the common good: "I believe it is acknowledged by all men of understanding that the strength and riches of a civil community, principally consists in the number of its free, virtuous and industrious inhabitants." Barrow doubted America could prosper if many of its residents were in chains.

He did not write primarily as an American, but as a Christian. The entire Bible levels a devastating critique of slavery. The tenor of the both the law and the gospel, Barrow insisted, made slavery "highly offensive to God."

Other pastors near Barrow's church disagreed. They poured out the cup of their fury on Barrow's head. These ministers formed a committee to investigate the activities of his little church before finally voting to remove his congregation from their association. The church's only crime was calling David Barrow to be its pastor. In response Barrow and a small handful of like-minded pastors formed a new network of churches committed to the cause of abolition.

Booth and Barrow are not remarkable for what they said. Many others in their generation had similar critiques. They are remarkable for where they said it: from behind a conservative, evangelical pulpit. Neither saw their words make an impact. Both died before their country changed course. They obviously didn't come to their position out of pragmatism but out of principle. They took a stand because they believed the Bible took a stand first.

The Way Forward

Our age calls for churches and pastors marked by prophetic compassion. This demands more than youthful zeal or naïve optimism. It requires the settled conviction that the Bible is Holy Scripture, the gospel is everyone's greatest need, and God's wisdom is worthy of public consumption.

The Bible is the very Word of God. It sets the agenda for every faithful, Christian ministry. The Bible will always be a better critic of contemporary society than our own consciences. It is, therefore, incumbent upon each church to affirm a commitment to speak where Scripture speaks and be silent where Scripture is silent. Both feats require careful discipline.

A church with a high view of Scripture will understand the centrality of the gospel. So long as the gospel is true, it is ultimately futile to save bodies from material poverty while leaving their spiritually impoverished souls unaddressed. The Christian lives with an eternal mindset. The next hundred years matter, this is true. But they pale in comparison to the next trillion. Let's agree that this world has value, God will renovate this earth by establishing the new earth. But let's not forget the only occupants of this heavenly city will be those who have bowed their knee to Christ the King. Social ministry without a call to repentance is, in the long run, worthless.

Make no mistake, churches with a high view of God's Word and God's gospel will have a high view of God, himself. They prize God's wisdom on every issue and will speak openly about the
private and social virtues that serve society best. Christians ought to share God's wisdom about gender, sex, marriage, life, and death. To be good and kind is to share this truth with others. Whether they accept this truth is up to them, but faithfulness demands we try. Abraham Booth and David Barrow had no power to change the laws of their country, they couldn't declare war, and they certainly couldn't change a human heart. But they could preach God's wisdom for humanity with the authority of God himself, and the same responsibility is given to every believer.

Moving forward our non-Christian neighbors may not adopt our evangelical position on the gospel, on abortion, on Islam, or on other biblical positions we take. Thankfully it is the Spirit's job to convict; ours is to reason. Where God has spoken we must speak, for this is how Christians "do good to everyone" (Galatians 6:10). It is our privilege to share the goodness of God lavishly and graciously, convinced his wisdom is what our neighbors desperately need both to live and to die well.

Aaron Menikoff (PhD, The Southern Baptist Theological Seminary) is senior pastor of Mt. Vernon Baptist Church in Atlanta, Georgia, and author of Politics and Piety (Pickwick. 2014). Before pastoral ministry, he served as an aide to United States Senator Mark O. Hatfield.

Christianity's Answer

"A Pharisee named Gamaliel . . .stood up in the Sanhedrin and ordered that the men be put outside. Then he addressed them: 'Men of Israel, consider carefully what you intend to do to these men . . .If their purpose is of human origin, it will fail. But if it is from God, you will not be able to stop these men; you will only find yourselves fighting against God."

ACTS 5: 33-39, NIV

Christianity's Answer

by Delber H. Elliott, D.D.

The dictators of the first century demanded of the early Christians that they must not teach nor preach in the name of Jesus. The answer of the Christians of that day was, "Whether it be right in the sight of God to hearken unto you more than unto God, judge ye. For we cannot but speak the things which we have seen and heart." For this answer these Christians were thrown into prison. When they were released the angel of the Lord told them to go and "speak to the people all the words of this life.: The dictators again forbade them. the answer of Peter and the other apostles was, "We ought to obey God rather than man."

In other words, if this is your command we must break it. If it is the mandate of your government we cannot respect it. Here we stand, let consequences be as they may! Since your orders are contrary to the will of God our allegiance must first be to God. For this answer James was beheaded, Stephen was stoned, Christ was crucified and multitudes have gone to prison and to death.

Christianity's answer has ever been the same. It was the answer of John Wyclif in England when he called the world back to the Scriptures by translating them into the English language. It was the answer of John Huss in Bohemia who was burned at the state for calling men back to Christ. It was the answer of Martin Luther when he called the people back to the cross and nailed his ninety-five theses to the Wittenburg chapel door. It was the answer of John Calvin when he called the church back to Christian doctrine and wrote his Institutes of Religion at the age of twenty-six. It was the answer John Knox who called the world back to the sovereignty of Christ over nations and withstood kings and queens who exercised despotic rule.

Scotland gave its final answer to the totalitarians just three hundred years ago when the National Covenant was subscribed and sworn by sixty thousand people in Greyfriars Church-yard in Edinburgh. The dictators were riding high. The Presbyterians were being forced to submit to the prelatic forms of worship.

The opposition, under the leadership of Alexander Henderson, drew up the document known as the National Covenant of Scotland. It was a declaration of independence of all dictators in church or state. As it was signed by the teeming thousands that day, some added the words, "until death".

This Covenant denounced the dictators of church and state. It gave no quarter to the state which sought to take over the church and use it for its own political ends. It also waged war against a dictatorship of the church over the state. No church must be allowed to take over the state and use it for its ecclesiastical ends. It furthermore gave no sanction to a dictatorship of a majority with God left out. It denied the right of the majority to whatever it desires regardless of whether it be right or wrong.

As one visits the battlefields of Bothwell Bridge, Drumclog and Ayrsmoss and reads the inscriptions upon their monuments as the writer has done he sees a little of what Scotland paid for its freedom. The stool of Janet Geddes is still on exhibition. The guillotine which cut of Argyle's head, the Tolbooth prison, the martyr memorial in Greyfriar's Churchyard are but a few of the reminders of a struggle which added thousands to the list of martyrs dead.

It gives one a weird sensation to go through the haunted halls of Holyrood Palace in Edinburgh where kings and queens reigned in all their totalitarian infamy. The spot is marked where Rizzio was murdered. The letter written by Mary Queen of Scots six hours before her execution is on exhibition. The audience room where Queen Mary had her arguments with John Knox is still preserved.

Knox seemed to be the one man whom Mary could not win by her charms. At last, impatient and angry she said "What have you to do with my affairs? What are you within this commonwealth?"

John Knox's answer was, "Madam, I am a subject born within the same. And albeit I neither be earl, lord, nor baron within it, yet has God made me a profitable member within the same." The church historian, Lindsay, says, "When John Knox uttered those words, modern democracy was born."

The world's answer to dictatorial aggression is force...Military power calls for military power to match it. There is truth in this of course. Germany could easily have been stopped when she first invaded the Rhineland.

But there is a further word which Christianity must speak. The mighty army of dictator aggression cannot be met by silence. This can bring only the peace of stagnation and death. It cannot be met by compromise with wrong. This only strengthens the power of the enemy for a future attack. Neither can it be conquered by material forces alone, for if these are inferior to those of the enemy what is our hope? It is only fighting fire with fire, with less of it. The deciding factor in the equation must be the spiritual. The final weapon must be the sword of the Spirit which is the Word of God, for we fight against the rulers of the darkness of this world.

From *The Trail of the Totalitarian*, Eerdmans Publishing Company, 1939

Delber H. Elliott, D.D. was Minister of the Central-Pittsburgh Reformed Presbyterian Church and author of: The Trail of Totalitarian, The Gospel According to Revelation, Doom of Dictators

Permission to use this excerpt given by Dr. Elliott's granddaughters: Kathy Stegall, Nancy Walton, Meg Garber.

"The Evil Empire" Speech

"How do you tell a communist? Well, it's someone who reads Marx and Lenin. And how do you tell an anti-Communist? It's someone who understands Marx and Lenin."

RONALD REAGAN

Remarks at the Annual Convention of the National Association of Evangelicals in Orlando, Florida March 8, 1983 ("The Evil Empire" Speech)

President Ronald Reagan

Reverend clergy all, Senator Hawkins, distinguished members of the Florida congressional delegation, and all of you:

I can't tell you how you have warmed my heart with your welcome. I'm delighted to be here today.

Those of you in the National Association of Evangelicals are known for your spiritual and humanitarian work. And I would be especially remiss if I didn't discharge right now one personal debt of gratitude. Thank you for your prayers. Nancy and I have felt their presence many times in many ways. And believe me, for us they've made all the difference.

The other day in the East Room of the White House at a meeting there, someone asked me whether I was aware of all the people out there who were praying for the President. And I had to say, "Yes, I am. I've felt it. I believe in intercessory prayer." But I couldn't help but say to that questioner after he'd asked the question that -- or at least say to them that if sometimes when he was praying he got a busy signal, it was just me in there ahead of him. [Laughter] I think I understand how Abraham Lincoln felt when he said, "I have been driven many times to my knees by the overwhelming conviction that I had nowhere else to go."

From the joy and the good feeling of this conference, I go to a political reception. [Laughter] Now, I don't know why, but that bit of scheduling reminds me of a story -- [laughter] -- which I'll share with you.

An evangelical minister and a politician arrived at Heaven's gate one day together. And St. Peter, after doing all the necessary formalities, took them in hand to show them where their quarters would be. And he took them to a small, single room with a bed, a chair, and a table and said this was for the clergyman. And the politician was a little worried about what might be in store for him. And he couldn't believe it then when St. Peter stopped in front of a beautiful mansion with lovely grounds, many servants, and told him that these would be his quarters.

And he couldn't help but ask, he said, "But wait, how -- there's something wrong -- how do I get this mansion while that good and holy man only gets a single room?" And St. Peter said, "You have to understand how things are up here. We've got thousands and thousands of clergy. You're the first politician who ever made it." [Laughter]

But I don't want to contribute to a stereotype. [Laughter] So, I tell you there are a great many God-fearing, dedicated, noble men and women in public life, present company included. And, yes, we need your help to keep us ever mindful of the ideas and the principles that brought us into the public arena in the first place. The basis of those ideals and principles is a commitment to freedom and personal liberty that, itself, is grounded in the much deeper realization that freedom prospers only where the blessings of God are avidly sought and humbly accepted.

The American experiment in democracy rests on this insight. Its discovery was the great triumph of our Founding Fathers, voiced by William Penn when he said: "If we will not be governed by God, we must be governed by tyrants." Explaining the inalienable rights of men, Jefferson said, "The God who gave us life, gave us liberty at the same time." And it was George

Washington who said that "of all the dispositions and habits which lead to political prosperity, religion and morality are indispensable supports."

And finally, that shrewdest of all observers of American democracy, Alexis de Tocqueville, put it eloquently after he had gone on a search for the secret of America's greatness and genius -- and he said: "Not until I went into the churches of America and heard her pulpits aflame with righteousness did I understand the greatness and the genius of America. . . . America is good. And if America ever ceases to be good, America will cease to be great."

Well, I'm pleased to be here today with you who are keeping America great by keeping her good. Only through your work and prayers and those of millions of others can we hope to survive this perilous century and keep alive this experiment in liberty, this last, best hope of man.

I want you to know that this administration is motivated by a political philosophy that sees the greatness of America in you, her people, and in your families, churches, neighborhoods, communities -- the institutions that foster and nourish values like concern for others and respect for the rule of law under God.

Now, I don't have to tell you that this puts us in opposition to, or at least out of step with, a prevailing attitude of many who have turned to a modern-day secularism, discarding the tried and time-tested values upon which our very civilization is based. No matter how well intentioned, their value system is radically different from that of most Americans. And while they proclaim that they're freeing us from superstitions of the past, they've taken upon themselves the job of superintending us by government rule and regulation. Sometimes their voices are louder than ours, but they are not yet a majority.

An example of that vocal superiority is evident in a controversy now going on in Washington. And since I'm involved, I've been waiting to hear from the parents of young America. How far are they willing to go in giving to government their prerogatives as parents?

Let me state the case as briefly and simply as I can. An organization of citizens, sincerely motivated and deeply concerned about the increase in illegitimate births and abortions involving girls well below the age of consent, sometime ago established a nationwide network of clinics to offer help to these girls and, hopefully, alleviate this situation. Now, again, let me say, I do not fault their intent. However, in their well-intentioned effort, these clinics have decided to provide advice and birth control drugs and devices to underage girls without the knowledge of their parents.

For some years now, the Federal Government has helped with funds to subsidize these clinics. In providing for this, the Congress decreed that every effort would be made to maximize parental participation. Nevertheless, the drugs and devices are prescribed without getting parental consent or giving notification after they've done so. Girls termed "sexually active" -- and that has replaced the word "promiscuous" -- are given this help in order to prevent illegitimate birth or abortion.

Well, we have ordered clinics receiving Federal funds to notify the parents such help has been given. One of the Nation's leading newspapers has created the term "squeal rule" in editorializing against us for doing this, and we're being criticized for violating the privacy of young people. A judge has recently granted an injunction against an enforcement of our rule. I've watched TV panel shows discuss this issue, seen columnists pontificating on our error, but no one seems to mention morality as playing a part in the subject of sex.

Is all of Judeo-Christian tradition wrong? Are we to believe that something so sacred can be looked upon as a purely physical thing with no potential for emotional and psychological harm? And isn't it the parents' right to give counsel and advice to keep their children from making mistakes that may affect their entire lives?

Many of us in government would like to know what parents think about this intrusion in their family by government. We're going to fight in the courts. The right of parents and the rights of family take precedence over those of Washington-based bureaucrats and social engineers.

But the fight against parental notification is really only one example of many attempts to water down traditional values and even abrogate the original terms of American democracy. Freedom prospers when religion is vibrant and the rule of law under God is acknowledged. When our Founding Fathers passed the first amendment, they sought to protect churches from government interference. They never intended to construct a wall of hostility between government and the concept of religious belief itself.

The evidence of this permeates our history and our government. The Declaration of Independence mentions the Supreme Being no less than four times. "In God We Trust" is engraved on our coinage. The Supreme Court opens its proceedings with a religious invocation. And the Members of Congress open their sessions with a prayer. I just happen to believe the schoolchildren of the United States are entitled to the same privileges as Supreme Court Justices and Congressmen.

Last year, I sent the Congress a constitutional amendment to restore prayer to public schools. Already this session, there's growing bipartisan support for the amendment, and I am calling on the Congress to act speedily to pass it and to let our children pray.

Perhaps some of you read recently about the Lubbock school case, where a judge actually ruled that it was unconstitutional for a school district to give equal treatment to religious and nonreligious student groups, even when the group meetings were being held during the students' own time. The first amendment never intended to require government to discriminate against religious speech.

Senators Denton and Hatfield have proposed legislation in the Congress on the whole question of prohibiting discrimination against religious forms of student speech. Such legislation could go far to restore freedom of religious speech for public school students. And I hope the Congress considers these bills quickly. And with your help, I think it's possible we could also get the constitutional amendment through the Congress this year.

More than a decade ago, a Supreme Court decision literally wiped off the books of 50 States statutes protecting the rights of unborn children. Abortion on demand now takes the lives of up to 1.5 million unborn children a year. Human life legislation ending this tragedy will some day pass the Congress, and you and I must never rest until it does. Unless and until it can be proven that the unborn child is not a living entity, then its right to life, liberty, and the pursuit of happiness must be protected.

You may remember that when abortion on demand began, many, and, indeed, I'm sure many of you, warned that the practice would lead to a decline in respect for human life, that the philosophical premises used to justify abortion on demand would ultimately be used to justify other attacks on the sacredness of human life -- infanticide or mercy killing. Tragically enough, those warnings proved all too true. Only last year a court permitted the death by starvation of a handicapped infant.

I have directed the Health and Human Services Department to make clear to every health care facility in the United States that the Rehabilitation Act of 1973 protects all handicapped persons against discrimination based on handicaps, including infants. And we have taken the further step of requiring that each and every recipient of Federal funds who provides health care services to infants must post and keep posted in a conspicuous place a notice stating that "discriminatory failure to feed and care for handicapped infants in this facility is prohibited by Federal law." It also lists a 24-hour, toll-free number so that nurses and others may report violations in time to save the infant's life.

In addition, recent legislation introduced in the Congress by Representative Henry Hyde of Illinois not only increases restrictions on publicly financed abortions, it also addresses this whole problem of infanticide. I urge the Congress to begin hearings and to adopt legislation that will protect the right of life to all children, including the disabled or handicapped.

Now, I'm sure that you must get discouraged at times, but you've done better than you know, perhaps. There's a great spiritual awakening in America, a renewal of the traditional values that have been the bedrock of America's goodness and greatness.

One recent survey by a Washington-based research council concluded that Americans were far more religious than the people of other nations; 95 percent of those surveyed expressed a belief in God and a huge majority believed the Ten Commandments had real meaning in their lives. And another study has found that an overwhelming majority of Americans disapprove of adultery, teenage sex, pornography, abortion, and hard drugs. And this same study showed a deep reverence for the importance of family ties and religious belief.

I think the items that we've discussed here today must be a key part of the Nation's political agenda. For the first time the Congress is openly and seriously debating and dealing with the prayer and abortion issues -- and that's enormous progress right there. I repeat: America is in the midst of a spiritual awakening and a moral renewal. And with your Biblical keynote, I say today, "Yes, let justice roll on like a river, righteousness like a never-failing stream."

Now, obviously, much of this new political and social consensus I've talked about is based on a positive view of American history, one that takes pride in our country's accomplishments and record. But we must never forget that no government schemes are going to perfect man. We know that living in this world means dealing with what philosophers would call the phenomenology of evil or, as theologians would put it, the doctrine of sin.

There is sin and evil in the world, and we're enjoined by Scripture and the Lord Jesus to oppose it with all our might. Our nation, too, has a legacy of evil with which it must deal. The glory of this land has been its capacity for transcending the moral evils of our past. For example, the long struggle of minority citizens for equal rights, once a source of disunity and civil war, is now a point of pride for all Americans. We must never go back. There is no room for racism, anti-Semitism, or other forms of ethnic and racial hatred in this country.

I know that you've been horrified, as have I, by the resurgence of some hate groups preaching bigotry and prejudice. Use the mighty voice of your pulpits and the powerful standing of your churches to denounce and isolate these hate groups in our midst. The commandment given us is clear and simple: "Thou shalt love thy neighbor as thyself."

But whatever sad episodes exist in our past, any objective observer must hold a positive view of American history, a history that has been the story of hopes fulfilled and dreams made into reality. Especially in this century, America has kept alight the torch of freedom, but not just for ourselves but for millions of others around the world.

And this brings me to my final point today. During my first press conference as President, in answer to a direct question, I pointed out that, as good Marxist-Leninists, the Soviet leaders have openly and publicly declared that the only morality they recognize is that which will further their cause, which is world revolution. I think I should point out I was only quoting Lenin, their guiding spirit, who said in 1920 that they repudiate all morality that proceeds from supernatural ideas -- that's their name for religion -- or ideas that are outside class conceptions. Morality is entirely subordinate to the interests of class war. And everything is moral that is necessary for the annihilation of the old, exploiting social order and for uniting the proletariat.

Well, I think the refusal of many influential people to accept this elementary fact of Soviet doctrine illustrates an historical reluctance to see totalitarian powers for what they are. We saw this phenomenon in the 1930's. We see it too often today.

This doesn't mean we should isolate ourselves and refuse to seek an understanding with them. I intend to do everything I can to persuade them of our peaceful intent, to remind them that it was the West that refused to use its nuclear monopoly in the forties and fifties for territorial gain and which now proposes 50-percent cut in strategic ballistic missiles and the elimination of an entire class of land-based, intermediate-range nuclear missiles.

At the same time, however, they must be made to understand we will never compromise our principles and standards. We will never give away our freedom. We will never abandon our belief in God. And we will never stop searching for a genuine peace. But we can assure none of these things America stands for through the so-called nuclear freeze solutions proposed by some.

The truth is that a freeze now would be a very dangerous fraud, for that is merely the illusion of peace. The reality is that we must find peace through strength.

I would agree to a freeze if only we could freeze the Soviets' global desires. A freeze at current levels of weapons would remove any incentive for the Soviets to negotiate seriously in Geneva and virtually end our chances to achieve the major arms reductions which we have proposed. Instead, they would achieve their objectives through the freeze.

A freeze would reward the Soviet Union for its enormous and unparalleled military buildup. It would prevent the essential and long overdue modernization of United States and allied defenses and would leave our aging forces increasingly vulnerable. And an honest freeze would require extensive prior negotiations on the systems and numbers to be limited and on the measures to ensure effective verification and compliance. And the kind of a freeze that has been suggested would be virtually impossible to verify. Such a major effort would divert us completely from our current negotiations on achieving substantial reductions.

A number of years ago, I heard a young father, a very prominent young man in the entertainment world, addressing a tremendous gathering in California. It was during the time of the cold war, and communism and our own way of life were very much on people's minds. And he was speaking to that subject. And suddenly, though, I heard him saying, "I love my little girls more than anything -- --" And I said to myself, "Oh, no, don't. You can't -- don't say that." But I had underestimated him. He went on: "I would rather see my little girls die now, still believing in God, than have them grow up under communism and one day die no longer believing in God."

There were thousands of young people in that audience. They came to their feet with shouts of joy. They had instantly recognized the profound truth in what he had said, with regard to the physical and the soul and what was truly important.

Yes, let us pray for the salvation of all of those who live in that totalitarian darkness -- pray they will discover the joy of knowing God. But until they do, let us be aware that while they preach the supremacy of the state, declare its omnipotence over individual man, and predict its eventual domination of all peoples on the Earth, they are the focus of evil in the modern world.

It was C. S. Lewis who, in his unforgettable "Screwtape Letters," wrote: "The greatest evil is not done now in those sordid 'dens of crime' that Dickens loved to paint. It is not even done in concentration camps and labor camps. In those we see its final result. But it is conceived and ordered (moved, seconded, carried and minuted) in clear, carpeted, warmed, and well-lighted offices, by quiet men with white collars and cut fingernails and smooth-shaven cheeks who do not need to raise their voice."

Well, because these "quiet men" do not "raise their voices," because they sometimes speak in soothing tones of brotherhood and peace, because, like other dictators before them, they're always making "their final territorial demand," some would have us accept them at their word and accommodate ourselves to their aggressive impulses. But if history teaches anything, it teaches that simple-minded appeasement or wishful thinking about our adversaries is folly. It means the betrayal of our past, the squandering of our freedom.

So, I urge you to speak out against those who would place the United States in a position of military and moral inferiority. You know, I've always believed that old Screwtape reserved his best efforts for those of you in the church. So, in your discussions of the nuclear freeze proposals, I urge you to beware the temptation of pride -- the temptation of blithely declaring yourselves above it all and label both sides equally at fault, to ignore the facts of history and the aggressive impulses of an evil empire, to simply call the arms race a giant misunderstanding and thereby remove yourself from the struggle between right and wrong and good and evil.

I ask you to resist the attempts of those who would have you withhold your support for our efforts, this administration's efforts, to keep America strong and free, while we negotiate real and verifiable reductions in the world's nuclear arsenals and one day, with God's help, their total elimination.

While America's military strength is important, let me add here that I've always maintained that the struggle now going on for the world will never be decided by bombs or rockets, by armies or military might. The real crisis we face today is a spiritual one; at root, it is a test of moral will and faith.

Whittaker Chambers, the man whose own religious conversion made him a witness to one of the terrible traumas of our time, the Hiss-Chambers case, wrote that the crisis of the Western World exists to the degree in which the West is indifferent to God, the degree to which it collaborates in communism's attempt to make man stand alone without God. And then he said, for Marxism-Leninism is actually the second oldest faith, first proclaimed in the Garden of Eden with the words of temptation, "Ye shall be as gods."

The Western World can answer this challenge, he wrote, "but only provided that its faith in God and the freedom He enjoins is as great as communism's faith in Man."

I believe we shall rise to the challenge. I believe that communism is another sad, bizarre chapter in human history whose last pages even now are being written. I believe this because the source of our strength in the quest for human freedom is not material, but spiritual. And because it knows no limitation, it must terrify and ultimately triumph over those who would enslave their fellow man. For in the words of Isaiah: "He giveth power to the faint; and to them that have no might He increased strength. . . . But they that wait upon the Lord shall renew their strength; they shall mount up with wings as eagles; they shall run, and not be weary. . . ."

Yes, change your world. One of our Founding Fathers, Thomas Paine, said, "We have it within our power to begin the world over again." We can do it, doing together what no one church could do by itself.

God bless you, and thank you very much.

Remarks at the Annual Convention of the National Association of Evangelicals in Orlando, Florida, 1983.
The Public Papers of President Ronald W. Reagan. Ronald Reagan Presidential Library.

Church Statism and the "Spirituality Doctrine"

"We sit by and watch the barbarian, we tolerate him; in the long stretches of peace we are not afraid. We are tickled by his irreverence, his comic inversion of our old certitudes and our fixed creed refreshes us; we laugh. But as we laugh we are watched by large and awful faces from beyond: and on these faces there is no smile."

HILAIRE BELLOC

Church Statism and the "Spirituality Doctrine"

By Charlie Rodriguez

S hould we be concerned that statist tendencies have infiltrated the Church? Yes, we should.

R.C. Sproul defines statism as a:

> ". . . philosophy or worldview. A decline from statehood
> to statism happens when the government is perceived
> as or claims to be the ultimate reality. This reality then
> replaces God as the supreme entity upon which human
> existence depends."

Like the individual and the state, the Church also has a philosophy or worldview. As such, a Church governmental structure (whether Episcopal, Presbyterian, Congregational) itself is not the revealed Word of God. So it stands to reason, because the structure (form of church government) itself is man-made, and not inerrant or infallible, that it too is subject to the consequences of sin.

The sin of statism in Church governments--including the doctrine of its spirituality--happens when that government "is perceived as or claims to be the ultimate reality," (Sproul) rather than the authority of Holy Scripture.

Beginning in the middle of the nineteenth century, with the issue of slavery as a hotly debated topic, church leaders began to take the position that the church should not involve itself in matters of the state—that it should concern itself with spiritual matters only. This position neatly allowed the church to support those in its membership who considered slaves as less than human.

During Civil Rights this same spirituality doctrine gave cover and justification for its non-involvement. Below is an understanding of the historical background and rationale used by the leadership of a prominent church (and there were many others) in order to justify its actions:

> In the summer of 1954, one prominent Southern Presbyterian church stood with its state legislature and the newly organized Citizens' Councils in their determination to challenge the federal ruling (Supreme Court, *Brown vs. Board of Education of Topeka, Kansas*) and defend white supremacy.

> No matter how erudite the arguments for segregation, and there were many, the strongest case against the Presbyterian church's denunciation of segregation still rested not in theological cases for segregation but in an appeal to the spirituality of the church. In 1957, in a carefully worded response to further pronouncements by the Council on Christian Relations, the church in question set out its case against the church's interference in the political issue of segregation:

> *The Session does not feel that the Presbyterian Church in the United States should take any action with reference to current social, political and economic problems . . . an organized church should exist only for the purpose of stimulating and strengthening its members and for coordinating and implementing their activities in bringing*

others to know Him and serve Him. (Peter Slade, *Open Friendship in a Closed Society*, p. 107, 108).

I keep a picture of Anne Moody, a beautiful 23 year old black student, who in 1963 dared to sit-in at a Woolworth lunch counter, to remind me of how sinful, misguided, and, yes, political the church can be at times by not following Christ. Following Christ means that we treat Anne Moody, who also was created in the image of God, with the same respect and dignity as we would a member of our own family or church. But as horrible as this scene was at Woolworths, it pales in comparison to something much more sinister and deep-routed as C.S. Lewis writes in Screwtape Letters:

> It is conceived and ordered (moved, seconded, carried and minuted) in clear, carpeted, warmed, and well-lighted offices, by quiet men with white collars and cut fingernails and smooth-shaven cheeks who do not need to raise their voice.

Today, as we look back at an ill-conceived and wrong church spirituality doctrine (example: maintaining that man-stealing and discrimination are just political issues that the church should not be involved in), one thing should be perfectly clear: A spirituality church doctrine, which is true to Scripture, should never be contrary to Scripture. Also, it should never prevent or intimidate (openly or subtlety) individual clergy and members from addressing, in or out of the Church, biblically-based moral issues (redefining marriage, abortion, stealing, lying, etc.) of our day, or of any day.

Not to do so is never sanctioned by Scripture. Never! Not to do so also allows the state and culture to define what is moral, or not, rather than a Holy God through Special Revelation. Thus, both the state's view apart from Scripture, and a Church doctrine which avoids "politicized moral issues"--but nonetheless biblically moral issues--these entities evolve very quickly into statist views. Why? Because "this reality then replaces God as the supreme entity upon which human existence depends." (Sproul)

So why do some churches, pastors, and theologians want to hold on to a spirituality doctrine which has caused so much grief and pain for almost two centuries? Is it nostalgia or ignorance or indifference? I don't know, and it's always been quite puzzling to me why some feel the need to defend it. But I do know this: a spirituality doctrine of this nature is where real tears need to be shed; it's where our anger should be; and it's where there is a greater degree of sin:

> Calvin and every one of the Reformers strenuously
> maintained that there is a difference between lesser sins and
> what they called gross and heinous sins. (R.C. Sproul, *Are
> There Degrees of Sin?*)

The historic "doctrine of the spirituality of the church" needs no proper burial service, metal casket, wreath, or eulogy. That would be offensive; but it does need to be buried, without delay, never to rise again.

Charlie Rodriguez, PCA Teaching Elder (Retired), Publisher and Literary Agent

When We Have No Recourse

"So the king of Jericho sent this message to Rahab: 'Bring out the men who came to you and entered your house, because they have come to spy out the whole land. But the woman had taken the two men and hidden them. She said, 'Yes, the men came to me, but I did not know where they had come from. At dusk, when it was time to close the city gate, the men left. I don't know which way they went. Go after them quickly. You may catch up with them.' (But she had taken them up to the roof and hidden them under the stalks of flax she had laid out on the roof.)"

JOSHUA 2:3-6

"A record of the genealogy of Jesus Christ the son of David, the son of Abraham . . .Salmon the father of Boaz, whose mother was Rahab, Boaz the father Obed, whose mother was Ruth."

MATTHEW 1:1, 5

When We Have No Recourse

by John M. Frame

Scripture tells us to respect those who rule over us, both in the church (Heb. 13:17) and in the state (Rom. 13:1-7, 1 Pet. 2:13-17). Rulers over the state during the NT period were, more often than not, non-Christian, but Paul and Peter teach that we owe obedience, honor, and deference, even to those rulers who do not share our faith. God gives us these rulers "to punish them who do evil and to praise those who do good" (1 Pet. 2: 14). Paul adds,

> For rulers are not a terror to good conduct, but to bad. Would you have no fear of the one who is in authority? Then do what is good, and you will receive his approval, ⁴ for he is God's servant for your good. But if you do wrong, be afraid, for he does not bear the sword in vain. For he is the servant of God, an avenger who carries out God's wrath on the wrongdoer. ⁵ Therefore one must be in subjection, not only to avoid God's wrath but also for the sake of conscience. (Rom 13:3-5)

So God has provided civil rulers as a service to us. They maintain a smoothly functioning society, discouraging crimes and providing justice for our good.

For that reason, Scripture is generally opposed to civil disobedience and revolution. After Peter affirms respect to civil rulers, he mentions analogous relationships (masters and slaves, husbands and wives) that are often painful because the ruler is cruel and oppressive. Even in these cases, Peter does not counsel rebellion, but he tells us to be like Christ in accepting suffering. It is a good thing, he says, when "one endures sorrows while suffering unjustly" (1 Pet. 2: 29). We should infer, then, that we should tolerate a certain amount of unjust suffering even from civil rulers, rather than resisting and rebelling against them.

But there are limits to such toleration. In Acts 4:18, the priests charged Peter and John "not to speak or teach at all in the name of Jesus." But they replied,

> "Whether it is right in the sight of God to listen to you rather
> than to God, you must judge, [20] for we cannot but speak of
> what we have seen and heard."
> (Acts 4:19)

The disciples therefore disobeyed the priestly orders, and the priests had them arrested again.

The narrative continues:

> And when they had brought them, they set them before the
> council. And the high priest questioned them, [28] saying, "We
> strictly charged you not to teach in this name, yet here you
> have filled Jerusalem with your teaching, and you intend to
> bring this man's blood upon us." [29] But Peter and the apostles
> answered, "We must obey God rather than men...
> (Acts 5:27-29)

The priests were among the rulers of the Jewish people, and they had soldiers at their disposal (Acts 5:26). Normally, Peter and John would have accepted their obligation to obey the commands of the priests; but in this case they declined. The priests had no right to silence the Gospel of Jesus Christ.

Is this the only exception to our obligation to obey rulers? I think not. Later in the Book of Acts, Paul was arrested again under the authority of Felix, the Roman governor of Caesarea. Felix was unconvinced by the evidence against Paul, but he kept Paul in prison, and after two years he was succeeded as governor by Porcius Festus (Acts 24:27). Shortly afterward, Paul was tried before Festus. He pled his innocence:

> But Paul said, "I am standing before Caesar's tribunal, where
> I ought to be tried. To the Jews I have done no wrong, as
> you yourself know very well. [11] If then I am a wrongdoer
> and have committed anything for which I deserve to die, I
> do not seek to escape death. But if there is nothing to their
> charges against me, no one can give me up to them. I appeal
> to Caesar." [12] Then Festus, when he had conferred with his
> council, answered, "To Caesar you have appealed; to Caesar
> you shall go." (Act 25:10-12)

Here we see Paul's subordination to civil magistrates and civil law, just as he recommends this to Christians in Rom. 13. He is willing to obey the law, even if the law prescribes death for him. But he is not willing to accept false charges against him. And he is willing to use provisions of the law to defend himself. As a Roman citizen, he has the right to appeal to the emperor himself, and he does.

Just as in modern nation-states, "obeying the law" can be a complicated business. For there are many administrators of the law, from Caesar, down to the Roman governors, down to the puppet kings (like Herod Agrippa, Acts 25:13-27), centurions, and soldiers. Any of these may order a person to do something, and their words are in effect law, at least for the moment. But of course all of these lawgivers are human beings, fallible, and sometimes wicked. These human lawgivers often make mistakes, and sometimes they willfully distort the legal process. To remedy such misuses of the law, most legal systems allow means of appeal to higher authorities. But to appeal to higher authority is to question, temporarily at least, the lower authority.

Does this mean that the highest civil authority, Caesar, is above the law, or that the law is whatever Caesar says it is? In most cases, no. The emperor or king is himself subject to other authorities, such as a legislature like the Roman Senate, or a system of courts. So we speak of "checks and balances." The society functions best when these authorities all operate within the boundaries of the law, resisting encroachments by other authorities.

When Paul tells Christians to be subject to authorities, he refers to that whole system of laws and appeals. It is that system that rewards good and punishes evil, even when an individual administrator fails or refuses to carry out his responsibility.

But what happens when the highest ruler, the emperor or king, becomes lawless? This is the definition of tyranny. In an otherwise well-ordered state, however, there is a remedy for that: what Calvin and the Reformed tradition have called the "lesser magistrates." In a well-ordered state, the Emperor or King may not do anything he likes. He is, like everyone else in the society, under law, the same law that everyone else must observe. The legislature, the courts, and the other administrators of the law have the right to call the Emperor or King to account. If he breaks the law, he must bear its punishment. In an extreme case, the law may provide that he be removed from office.

Of course, all this is more easily said than done. Emperors, Kings, and Presidents often do not respond gladly to those who attempt to enforce a nation's laws against them. Frequently, the misbehavior of the highest magistrate leads to a "constitutional crisis." And often the written statutes of the law do not tell the society what to do in a constitutional crisis. Even the most well-ordered society can be broken down by the efforts of sinful rulers.

And so we should consider the "worst-case scenario," a system like that of Nazi Germany in which the state, instead of being a terror to bad conduct (Rom. 13:3) becomes a terror to the good. In such a terror state, all mechanisms of appeal break down, and an evil ruler enforces his arbitrary ability to arrest or kill anyone who gets in his way.

Such a state, in my judgment, is not a "governing authority" "instituted by God" in terms of Rom. 13:1. But even in this sort of situation we ought to observe the respect for authority that we have seen in Rom. 13 and 1 Pet. 2. We should never be anarchists, people who reject all authority in favor of their own autonomy. We should seek to form something better. We should gather together in a group that has the goal of being a functional government. That embryo government must seek justice. That group may, and should, become a fighting force; for that is one of the important functions of government, to defend its society by force if necessary.

The terror state will not acknowledge the legitimacy of our embryo government. They, and uncommitted people in the society, may well characterize it as a rebellion or a revolutionary movement. They may invoke against it the passages we cited earlier, from Rom. 13 and 1 Pet. 2. Ultimately, God will judge.

In the Viet Nam war, there was often confusion as to who was the "legitimate government" in a territory. In a village, the Saigon government might establish rule during the day, while the Viet Cong would rule at night. Christians were faced with the question of which of these, or a third, was a legitimate government in terms of Rom. 13. Sometimes the question did not have an obvious answer. But Christians were forced to pray for wisdom to gain God's answer, and then to act accordingly.

So there are times when God authorizes Christians to be part of what some would characterize as a rebellion or revolution against a state. We should not enter lightly into such a movement. It can be a matter of life and death. And we should approach such a decision with a keen sense of our own sin, our need of God's grace in Christ, and prayer for the wisdom of God's Holy Spirit.

John M. Frame (AB, Princeton; BD, Westminster Theological Seminary' MA and MPhil, Yale; DD, Belhaven) holds the J.D. Trimble Chair of Systematic Theology and Philosophy at Reformed Theological Seminary in Orlando and is the author of many books, including the four-volume Theology of Lordship series.

The Paris Attacks

Understanding the Psychology of Ideological Mass Murder and What We Can do About It

"When justice is done, it brings joy to the righteous but terror to evildoers."

PROVERBS 21:15

The Paris Attacks:
Understanding the Psychology
of Ideological Mass Murder
and What We Can do About It

Interview with Dr. Michael Welner, Forensic Psychiatrist

Effective Psychiatric Treatment welcomes Dr. Michael Welner, Chairman of The Forensic Panel and one of America's most accomplished forensic psychiatrists. Dr. Welner has consulted on numerous mass killings, most recently the Aurora movie theater shooting in Colorado. He has been a key contributor to landmark Congressional legislation (HR 2646) to dramatically upgrade crisis psychiatry intervention. Dr. Welner is responsible for a number of innovations in forensic science. His research includes online surveys in which the public– including psychiatrists– collectively contribute to efforts to weigh the severity of crimes by intent, actions, and attitudes. He encourages everyone to participate and involve others in this important effort at www.depravitystandard.org.

Dr. Deitz: Dr. Welner, Thank you for your time. Can you briefly describe the types of mass murder and where the Paris and Mali attacks fit into the overall schema?

Dr. Welner: Experience leads me to distinguish six types of mass killers:

1. Community–random targeting seeking to maximize death
2. Ideological—either targeting symbols or prejudices for

       ideological statement, or seeking to maximize number of
       deaths to promote a cause
3. Workplace—targeting a workplace, usually its leadership
4. School—targeting classmates, teachers, and sources of
     conflict
5. Family—annihilation in the context of unexpected financial
     collapse,
6. finality of divorce, abandonment)
7. Criminal—drug-gang violence, robberies

The Paris and Mali tragedies demonstrate the qualities of Ideological Mass Killing.

Dr. Deitz: Where do Ideological mass killings fit in among the above categories?

Dr. Welner: Ideological mass killings in America involve those who employ an issue-agenda to paper over longstanding homicidal fantasies. Recognizing the wrong of killing a complete stranger, a person may be indoctrinated (as occurs in some U.S. prisons or in a subset of ideologically-sympathetic mosques) or self-indoctrinate (through social networking) to dehumanize the nominal enemy, be it the police, racial or religious minorities, the military, or those of different cultures. The process of indoctrination for such turbulent characters dehumanizes a class of victims to the end that the aspiring killers truly believe that such individuals deserve to die in order to create spectacle.

Dr. Deitz: How do the Events of Paris and Mali differ from other mass murders that have occurred recently in the United Sates?
Dr. Welner: American mass killers are far more frequently driven by the psychological motivation to transcend into larger than life anti-heroes, airbrushed by sentimental media portrayals that amplify their humanity precisely because they have undertaken the inhumane. Those victims unrelated to the "cause" who are killed or wounded are ultimately regarded as collateral damage, once the killer becomes invested in creating spectacle at all costs.

Dr. Deitz: Are the Jihadist terrorist attacks as carried out in Paris and Mali a different animal?

Dr. Welner: The Paris and Mali attacks differ from many of the ideological mass killings in America in their execution by a trained paramilitary force far more committed to a collective cause, compared to the glory-seeking of American social failures who are seduced by the vanity of their portrayal after the fact. The pathway of those recruited to coordinated activity, be it in Paris or September 11, reflects more upon the personal success and selection of jihadists because of their capabilities rather than the failure and disenfranchisement of the dead-ender who massacres to demonstrate Jihadist sympathies (such as Nidal Hassan, who murdered 13 people at Fort Hood, Texas).

Dr. Deitz: Dr. Welner, you have had extensive experience interviewing ideological mass murderers. What have you learned about the evolution of their attitudes? Can psychiatry help?

Dr. Welner: Mass killing of all types is the endpoint of a clinical pathway involving a sequence of twelve steps:

> **First**: Externalizing blame—it is always someone else's fault when things don't go well
> **Second**: High or patchy self-esteem—expectations of greatness
> **Third**: Poor characterological resilience—difficulty rebounding from adversity
> **Fourth**: Social rejection, particularly psychosexual rejection
> **Fifth**: Identification with potency of destructiveness— destruction force perceived as power
> **Sixth**: Identification with destructive icons
> **Seventh**: isolation and psychosexual incompetence— with very few exceptions, solitary mass murderers are heterosexual men
> **Eighth**: Identifying with alienation—embracing alienation in order to blame the rejecting outer world for failures

Ninth: Failures mount to a degree that they predict further and future failure
Tenth: Anger and alienation directed to destructive fantasy
Eleventh: Hopelessness inspires destructive alternative identity and a concrete plan
And finally: Investment in achieving the destructive mission—the ultimate ambition

Clinical intervention to redirect the evolving homicidality of a prospective killer can occur at any time along this path until the end-stage. At that point, the prospective killer becomes so mobilized around a destructive plan that any intervention is perceived as an obstacle to his psychological needs. That is the point of no return; if we look at the killer as a potentially explosive bomb, this is the point beyond which the fuse has been lit.

Dr. Deitz: Is there any intervention other than guns, bomb-sniffing dogs and metal detectors to protect against these sorts of acts?

Dr. Welner: In contemporary America and other fame-driven cultures, there is tremendous social incentive for alienated and violently-identified young males who have given up on achieving once-lofty ambition to opt for destructiveness. That incentive is created and perpetuated by 24-hour news media, which conveys a platform for mass killers to refashion themselves into icons for their ideological fellow travelers.

ISIS's social incentives for mass killing mirror those codified by the Palestinian Authority, which financially rewarded and memorialized suicide bombers targeting Jews with the greatest distinction, including religious deification. Such unmatched frequency of mass murder of civilians by civilians requires more than a news media; it connotes a concerted coordination between political authority, religious leadership, and hermetically controlled mass-media. The required social incentives have to be more powerful than misery and poverty (a ubiquitous global problem), or even tribal strife (numerous areas in the developing world) or powerlessness (Tibet, Burma, American Indians).

Socioculturally, the best chance to eliminate ideological mass murder as a life choice is to extinguish its social incentives. The mass media has the capacity to portray ideological mass murder as the ultimate perversion. Over the years, the mass media demonized and socially rejected bigotry based on race and sexual orientation to the degree that such intolerance and insensitivity has been systematically eradicated in the West. Until such forces are marshaled against ideological mass killers, the quest for spectacle through destructiveness will only worsen.

Regarding Jihadism, the responsibility for eliminating Jihadist mass murder lies within the Muslim community itself. Until the Muslim community mobilizes and emphatically ridicules and humiliates rejectionist and nihilistic elements into stopping mass killing, the problem will grow and spread – in Muslim countries and secular countries alike. The rejection of spectacle Jihadist murder can only be achieved when responsible people empower and embolden those pluralistic Muslims who are courageous enough to denounce the nihilistic element of Islam. Humor is an underutilized weapon, but as Charlie Hebdo proved before its decimation, a very impactful one. Humiliated individuals like racist Donald Sterling and sexual predator Jerry Sandusky attract no followers.

Metal detectors may interrupt a plot in motion. Gun regulations will create obstacles for those isolated loners attempting to kill on a grander scale, but will create gun-free killing fields for others integrated enough into terror networks to arm themselves despite regulations (such as in Paris).

Eliminating the social incentive to mass killing is a clinical imperative for mental health professionals who may encounter young men wrestling with destructive choices which they appraise to be all too realistic.

Dr. Deitz: Thank you, Dr. Welner.

Dr. Welner: You are welcome. Thank you for inviting me.

Dr. Michael Welner is Chairman of The Forensic Panel and one of America's most accomplished forensic psychiatrists. Dr. Welner has consulted on numerous mass killings, most recently the Aurora movie theater shooting in Colorado. He has been a key contributor to landmark Congressional legislation (HR 2646) to dramatically upgrade crisis psychiatry intervention. Dr. Welner is responsible for a number of innovations in forensic science. His research includes online surveys in which the public– including psychiatrists– collectively contribute to efforts to weigh the severity of crimes by intent, actions, and attitudes.

Benevolent Bondage

"Every step which leads from capitalism toward planning is necessarily a step nearer to absolutism and dictatorship."

Benevolent Bondage

by Frank Wright, Ph.D.

Abraham Lincoln at Gettysburg expressed the hope that the lives of those who gave "the last full measure of their devotion" would inspire a new birth of freedom. Instead, these many years later, it seems Americans stand on the threshold of a new birth of *statism*, as we witness the greatest expansion of government power in the history of our nation.

Emblematic of this massive expansion is the federal government's assertion of authority over the entire healthcare industry. Using its newfound leverage, the government is shaping a forced national policy in areas like: abortion, contraception, and euthanasia. Unsurprisingly, this coercive statism is accompanied by limitations on personal freedoms and significant new tax burdens.

Some view the magnitude and scope of this expansion of state control as a pathway to tyranny. Those more sanguine see a strong government as better able to provide for the common good. Which is it?

We find a helpful biblical perspective in a familiar narrative—the memorable story of Joseph in Egypt. Some see this account as an example of a powerful and benevolent government helping people survive a great calamity. But a closer look is instructive.

In Genesis 41, Joseph is released from prison to interpret Pharaoh's dream. The dream was of seven fat cows and seven ears of plump grain, followed by seven thin, sickly cows and seven ears of blighted grain.

Joseph's interpretation of the dream as seven years of abundance followed by seven years of famine, along with his proposed solution, gains immediate favor with Pharaoh. So under Pharaoh's authority, Joseph <u>confiscates</u> one-fifth of all the grain in the land; then we read these ominous words: *The seven years of famine began to come.*

With the famine upon them, deprivation followed. Joseph then opened the storehouses and <u>sold</u> grain back to the Egyptians—the very grain Pharaoh previously confiscated.

For most, this is where the story ends. Because of Joseph's wisdom and favor with God, a great disaster is averted. But stopping here, we miss a crucial part of the story found in Genesis 47.

In a description difficult to comprehend in our day, the biblical text is blunt: *there was no food in all the land.* And then something equally blunt: *Joseph gathered up <u>all</u> the money in Egypt in exchange for grain.*

With the famine undiminished, the people were forced to return to Joseph for more food. This time he took <u>all</u> their livestock in exchange for food—that livestock being the very means of production in an agrarian economy.

Still in the grip of the famine, the people came back the following year for more food. This time the people asked Joseph to buy their land and *themselves* for food. So the money, the livestock, and the land are now Pharaoh's—and the people are his servants.

From being free landowners, the people effectively became indentured sharecroppers, with Pharaoh continuing to take 1/5 of the grain. Interestingly, the priests were excluded—not only keeping their land, but also receiving an allowance from Pharaoh, and revealing how easily religious leaders can be co-opted.

Stopping here with the narrative, we should note three things. First, in their desperation the Egyptian people willingly agreed to everything. Second, with the famine over, the people remained in bondage. Third, when next we see the Israelites in Exodus chapter one, they are all slaves.

So under the all-powerful (and seemingly benevolent) government of Pharaoh, the people survived the catastrophic famine. But they also went:

> From freedom to crisis;
> From crisis to benevolent bondage; and
> From benevolent bondage to servitude.

Said another way, any government powerful enough to give you everything you need is powerful enough to take away everything you have.

Remembering our own fallen condition, what can we learn about ourselves from this narrative? At least two things, I think. First, we are sometimes little different from the Egyptians, with a propensity to live by sight and not by faith. And second, we too are often willing to exchange freedom for security.

The larger question then becomes: Is that where we are today? With the rising statism in our day, are we standing at the threshold of a benevolent bondage? For the people of God, this is no small matter, as far more would be lost in such bondage than just personal freedom.

If we put our trust in "princes," lost is the veracity of our faith witness before a watching world. Lost is the joy of seeing God provide, sometimes miraculously. Lost is the intimacy of our relationship with him, as we look to another to provide. Lost also is the sense of purpose that comes from being part of His divine plan.

Standing on the battlefield at Gettysburg, Lincoln spoke of a new birth of freedom for a nation under God, reminding us there is only one form of bondage that is truly benevolent. It is bondage to the Great King, who spared not His own Son but delivered Him up for us all—that we might be loosed from our sins in His own precious blood.

Dr. Wright holds a Ph.D. in Finance from Florida Atlantic University and is an ordained Elder in the Presbyterian Church in America. He established the Center for Christian Statesmanship as a vital force for evangelism and the biblical worldview on Capitol Hill; served for over a decade as the President and CEO of the National Religious Broadcasters; former President and COO of Salem Communications Corporation; joined D. James Kennedy Ministries as President and CEO on April 15, 2015.

Why the Peaceful Majority
is Irrelevant

"Socialism may be established by force, as in the Soviet Socialist Republics—or by vote, as in Nazi (National Socialist) Germany. The degree of socialization may be total, as in Russia—or partial, as in England. Theoretically, the differences are superficial; practically, they are only a matter of time. The basic principle, in all cases, is the same."

AYN RAND

Why the Peaceful Majority is Irrelevant

by Paul Marek

I used to know a man whose family were German aristocracy prior to World War Two. They owned a number of large industries and estates. I asked him how many German people were true Nazis, and the answer he gave has stuck with me and guided my attitude toward fanaticism ever since.

"Very few people were true Nazis" he said, "but, many enjoyed the return of German pride, and many more were too busy to care. I was one of those who just thought the Nazis were a bunch of fools. So, the majority just sat back and let it all happen. Then, before we knew it, they owned us, and we had lost control, and the end of the world had come. My family lost everything. I ended up in a concentration camp and the Allies destroyed my factories."

We are told again and again by "experts" and "talking heads" that Islam is the religion of peace, and that the vast majority of Muslims just want to live in peace. Although this unquantified assertion may be true, it is entirely irrelevant. It is meaningless fluff, meant to make us feel better, and meant to somehow diminish the specter of fanatics rampaging across the globe in the name of Islam. The fact is, that the fanatics rule Islam at this moment in history. It is the fanatics who march. It is the fanatics who wage any one of 50 shooting wars world wide. It is the fanatics who systematically slaughter Christian or tribal groups throughout Africa and are gradually taking over the entire continent in an Islamic wave. It is the fanatics who bomb, behead, murder, or honor kill. It is the fanatics who take over mosque after mosque. It is the fanatics who zealously spread the stoning and hanging of rape victims and homosexuals. The hard quantifiable fact is, that the "peaceful majority" is the "silent majority" and it is cowed and extraneous.

Communist Russia was comprised of Russians who just wanted to live in peace, yet the Russian Communists were responsible for the murder of about 20 million people. The peaceful majority were irrelevant. China's huge population was peaceful as well, but Chinese Communists managed to kill a staggering 70 million people. The average Japanese individual prior to World War II was not a war mongering sadist. Yet, Japan murdered and slaughtered its way across South East Asia in an orgy of killing that included the systematic killing of 12 million Chinese civilians; most killed by sword, shovel, and bayonet. And, who can forget Rwanda, which collapsed into butchery. Could it not be said that the majority of Rwandans were "peace loving".

History lessons are often incredibly simple and blunt, yet for all our powers of reason we often miss the most basic and uncomplicated of points. Peace-loving Muslims have been made irrelevant by the fanatics. Peace-loving Muslims have been made irrelevant by their silence. Peace-loving Muslims will become our enemy if they don't speak up, because like my friend from Germany, they will awake one day and find that the fanatics own them, and the end of their world will have begun. Peace-loving Germans, Japanese, Chinese, Russians, Rwandans, Bosnians, Afghans, Iraqis, Palestinians, Somalis, Nigerians, Algerians, and many others, have died because the peaceful majority did not speak up until it was too late. As for us who watch it all unfold, we must pay attention to the only group that counts; the fanatics who threaten our way of life.

Paul Marek was born in Winnipeg, Manitoba, Canada in 1957. Throughout his life he worked as a teacher, an educational consultant, freelance writer, and owner of a wilderness lodge. Marek's lifelong passion has been reading history, especially that of the Second World War. The community that he grew up in was a melting pot of European immigrants, where Germans, Ukrainians, Czechs, Poles, and others had to learn to live side by side and bury the animosities of Old Europe. Marek gained much insight into the Second World War by speaking with its survivors from both sides of the conflict. There were farmers who had seen their neighbors become victims of the holocaust, German industrialists who lost everything, and even family members who had participated in the Czech reprisals. These conversations, coupled with the reading of history texts, have worked to formulate Marek's views on contemporary geopolitics. Currently Paul Marek works as an Educational Consultant in Saskatoon, Canada.

Church and State

"Bring us back. Bring a great revival to this land."

D. JAMES KENNEDY

Church and State

by D. James Kennedy

Text: "Render therefore unto Caesar the things which are Caesar's and unto God the things that are God's."
Matthew 22:21

One issue which most perplexes and troubles our national life today, publicly and privately, is the issue of church and state. Few people have missed reading about some, of the battles waged over this issue. Before the Congress of the United States are several bills dealing with the pros and cons of this issue; a number of cases dealing with this subject are being heard before courts at various levels across this nation; numerous speeches have been made; organizations have been formed—all in the effort to either further separate or further unite the religions of the people to the government and public life of this nation.

Let no one be historically benighted about the First Amendment to our Constitution. It is from the Bill of Rights and states that Congress shall make no law respecting the establishment of religion or forbidding the free exercise thereof. That is the establishment and exercise of religion amendment to the Constitution. It has been reduced to a cliché, namely, the separation of church and state. The question is: what precisely does that mean?

The Real Meaning of Separation

A great deal of ink has flowed over that particular question. Some prefer that separation to be absolute: no relationship whatsoever between the government and the church, religion, or God. People with any sympathetic understanding of the desires and ideals of the Founding Fathers know they did not have that in mind. Moreover, to forbid the establishment of a religion has never meant to sever any relationship between government and God.

Historically, whether or not to establish a state religion, as the Church of England has been in England, has been at the heart of the battle in the United States. In our youth we probably learned what the longest word in the dictionary was at one time: antidisestablishmentarianism. It described this whole problem of either establishing or disestablishing a church as the official state church. It was not concerned with whether to sever God from the national life or not. However, many persons today are powerfully organized and engaged in making it mean precisely that.

A number of years ago before the Supreme Court, Madalyn Murray O'Hair successfully fought to remove voluntary praying and Scripture reading from public school classrooms. For the most part, that court decision has been carried out. Now she is litigating for the accomplishment of the next items on her atheistic agenda such as removing the national motto "In God We Trust" from our coins and from our currency, and also the words "Under God" from the Pledge of Allegiance. After those battles, a whole list of more items lies ready to be acted upon.

Many people, including Christians, are obscure on what the relationship between church and state should be. Many have fallen prey to the propaganda that, by its antiestablishment clause, the Constitution has meant there should be no relationship between God or Christianity and the government. Some of you believe that. No assertion could be further from the historical facts!

After the first service this morning, a young lady made some very interesting comments to me. Being a teacher, she had been educated to instruct our children. She told me that she never before had heard most of the things I said in the first service. She was astounded that she could be educated in this country, yet be almost completely oblivious to the facts which I brought to light. Some of you may be equally surprised.

While presenting documentation, I would ask you simply to consider this question: Did the founders of this nation intend it to be a secularist, neutral, humanist nation; or did they believe that this was a nation created to the glory of God and that it was to be a godly, Christian state? So pervasive has been the propaganda for the first view listed that probably in hearing that last statement, some of you are saying, "Why, of course not. We are to be neutral!" Is it so? I will present the evidence to you, and you can draw your own conclusions.

The Christian Roots of America

The first settlement in this country was the one at Jamestown in 1607. Even before the settlers left England, they drew up the First Charter of Virginia, the official document providing for the settlement of Jamestown. In it we find the first beginnings of America. Dated 1606, the Charter nobly declares that "We greatly commending, and graciously accepting of, their Desires for the Furtherence of so noble a work, which may, by the Province of Almighty God, hereafter tend to the Glory of His Divine Majesty, in propagating the Christian Religion to such People, as yet live in Darkness and miserable ignorance of the true Knowledge and Worship of God, and may in time bring the infidels and Savages, living in those Parts, to human Civility, and to a settled and quiet Government...."

You might want to learn about the first act performed by the settlers who founded the Jamestown colony. First thing after they had landed at Cape Henry in April of 1607, they erected a large wooden cross and held a prayer meeting! That first act in this new land, my friend, was on *publicly chartered* land!

Next, chronologically, the Pilgrims sailed on the Mayflower to land at Plymouth Rock. On November 11, 1620, as their ship lay offshore, before they set foot on this new continent, the Pilgrims joined together and signed the Mayflower Compact. This Compact of the first permanent settlement in this land begins with these words: "In the name of God, Amen." It continues "Having undertaken for the gloire of God, and advancements of the Christian faith, and honour of our king and countries a voyage to plant the first colonie in the Northerne parts of Virginia, doe by these presents solemnly and mutualy in the presence of God, and one of another, covenant and combine ourselves together into a civil body politick ..."

Governor William Bradford described the first thing the Pilgrims did when they landed on these shores. He wrote, "Being thus arrived in a good harbor and brought safe to land, they fell upon their knees and blessed the God of Heaven..."

The first written constitution which created a government in this land was the Fundamental Orders of Connecticut in 1639. This first constitution written in America includes these words "Forasmuch as it hath pleased the Allmighty God by the wise disposition of his divine providence so to Order and dispose of things... " It continues, "And well knowing where a people are gathered together the word of God requires that to mayntayne the peace and union of such a people there should be an orderly and decent Government established according to God..." It further states that "... to mayntayne and preserve the liberty and purity of the Gospell of our Lord Jesus which we now professes as also the discipline of the Churches, which according to the truth of the said gospell is now practised amongst us..."

That brings us next to May 19,1643, when, under heavy attack, the early settlers of this country joined together to form the New England Confederation, the first confederation of the various communities of "New England," as this land was then called. Its document begins with these words: "Whereas we all came into these parts of America with one and the same end and aim, namely, to advance the Kingdom of our Lord Jesus Christ and to enjoy the liberties of the Gospel in the purity with peace..."

The first Pennsylvania Charter of Privileges reads thusly, "...And Almighty God being the only Lord of Conscience, Father of Lights and

Spirits; and the Author as well as Object of all divine Knowledge, Faith and Worship, who only doth enlighten the Minds, and persuade and convince the Understanding of People ..." it concludes: "And that all Persons who also profess to believe in Jesus Christ, the Saviour of the World, shall be capable (not withstanding their other Persuasions and Practices in Point of Conscience and Religion) to serve this Government in any Capacity, both legislatively and executivley ..."

Freedom by the Providence of God

In the providence of God there came forth the Declaration of independence, which includes in its first paragraph an appeal to the laws of nature and of nature's God. In the second paragraph we find these famous words: "We hold these truths to be self-evident, that all men are created equal, that they are endowed by their Creator with certain unalienable rights, that among these are Life, Liberty, and the pursuit of Happiness."

Notice it says that all men are *created* equal. It does not say that they evolved equally. They are endowed by their *Creator*, not by the primeval slime, with certain unalienable rights. Is it not a strange turn of events that a nation born of the Declaration should have come to a place where it is illegal to teach in our schools that we have been created by a divine Creator.

Humanistic, atheistic secularism has become in effect the religion of our land. Creation may not be taught in the schools created by this Declaration. Hopefully, the time is not far off when someone will have the courage to take this situation to the courts and challenge it. Twice the Supreme Court has declared that humanism is a religion, yet it continues to be taught as the very fact, fabric, substance and substratum of all our education. When shall we stand up and say, "No more!"?

The Declaration of Independence concludes, "And for the support of this Declaration, with a firm reliance on the protection of divine Providence, we mutually pledge to each other our Lives, our Fortunes, and our sacred Honor."

Finally, we come to the formation of the Constitution. The representatives had been meeting together for three weeks, struggling and wrestling to come up with something. They had surveyed all the governments of Europe but had found nothing that would suffice. Finally, having made little or no progress, an elderly gentleman stood up and looked through his spectacles at them. His name was Benjamin Franklin. (This man is often accused of simply being a deist. A deist believes that God has nothing to do with the affairs of men, that He is an "absentee landlord" who winds the clock and lets it run down, that He certainly does not answer prayers or deal with providence.) Franklin plainly said in the convention that met to draw up the Constitution, "I have lived, Sir, a long time, and the longer I live, the more convincing proofs I see of this truth—that God governs in the affairs of men. And if a sparrow cannot fall to the ground without His Notice, is it probable that an empire can rise without His aid? We have been assured, Sir, in the sacred writings, that 'Except the Lord build the house, they labor in vain that build it.' I firmly believe this; and I also believe that without His concurring aid we shall succeed in this political building no better than the builders of Babel."

From the Beginning a Call to God

George Washington who, according to his own prayer diary, was unquestionably a Christian, assumed the first presidency of this nation. In his first inaugural address he said, "It would be peculiarly improper to omit in this first official act my fervent supplications to that Almighty Being who rules over the universe, who presides in the councils of nations ... In tendering this homage to the Great Author of every public and private good, I assure myself that it expresses your sentiments not less than my own ..." He finished, saying, "I shall take my present leave; but not without resorting once more to the benign Parent of the Human Race in humble supplication that, since He has been pleased to favor the American people with opportunities ... so His divine blessing may be equally conspicuous in the enlarged views, the temperate consultations, and the wise measure on which the success of this Government must depend."

One of his early official acts was the First Thanksgiving Proclamation which reads, "Whereas it is the duty of all nations to acknowledge the providence of Almighty God, to obey His will, to be grateful for His benefits, and humbly implore His protection and favor..." it goes on to call the nation to thankfulness to Almighty God.

All the Presidents refer to the Almighty God, who is Author of Our liberty, or to His providence, upon which our hopes depend, in their inaugural addresses. As I read these all recently, I was impressed that down through the years and centuries, President after President, without exception, made references or appeals in their inaugural addresses to the aid of Almighty God to fulfill the offices which they held.

In reading over the Constitutions of all 50 of our states, I discovered something which some of you may not know there is *in all 50, without exception,* an appeal or a prayer to the Almighty God of this universe. In testimony and evidence of that I quote the following "We, the people of the State of North Carolina, grateful to Almighty God, the Sovereign Ruler of Nations, for the preservation of the American Union and the existence of our civil, political and religious liberties ..." The Constitution of the State of Vermont says, "That all men have a natural and unalienable right to worship Almighty God according to the dictates of their own consciences ..." That of the State of New York says, "We, the People of the State of New York, grateful to Almighty God for our Freedom, in order to secure its blessings, DO ESTABLISH THIS CONSTITUTION." Through all 50 state Constitutions, without exception, there runs this same appeal and reference to God who is the Creator of our liberties and the preserver of our freedoms.

Monumental Evidence

Having looked at the documents by which our land was founded, the inaugural addresses of all the Presidents, and the Constitutions of all 50 of our states, I was brought at last to look at the monumental evidence in Washington, D. C. I am particularly thankful for it to Dr Hodge, who had done a wonderful work at the end of the last century, and also more recently to Dr. Weiss, who had made an outstanding collection of evidence of this sort.

If you were to look at the various national buildings and monuments in the capital of this nation, you would find unimpeachable evidence of the official commitment of this land to a belief in the living God, the Word of God, and His Son Jesus Christ.

For example, hovering over our nation's capital is that magnificent Capitol building, a symbol of the national life of our land. The cornerstone had been laid by George Washington himself. Later a box containing a number of documents was inserted, including a manuscript in the handwriting of Daniel Webster, Secretary of State of the United States, which concluded, "And all here assembled, whether belonging to public life or to private life, with hearts devotedly thankful to Almighty God for the preservation of the liberty and happiness of the country, unite in sincere and fervent prayer that this deposit and the walls and arches, the domes and towers, the columns and the entablatures, now to be erected over it, may endure forever. God save the United States of America."

If you were to go into the House of Representatives and look above the chair where the one who presides over that house sits, you would find in large words etched in the marble our official national motto, *approved by the Senate and by the House of Representatives*: IN GOD WE TRUST.

You may then want to go and sit in on the Supreme Court and listen to its proceedings. Before they begin their deliberations, the crier comes forth, and his voice shouts these official words: "Oyez! Oyez! Oyez! All persons having business before the Honorable, the Supreme Court of the United States, are admonished to draw near and give their attention, for the court is now sitting. God save the United States and the Honorable Court." I am afraid, however, that since those words were first penned, different sentiments have crept into that Court. Maybe we should have the crier cry instead, "God save the United States *from* this Supreme Court."

Enter the White House, where our President lives, and see the words placed over the fireplace by the first President to inhabit that building, John Adams, which says, "I pray Heaven to bestow the best of Blessings on this [White] House and on all that shall hereafter inhabit it ..."

Go then to that monument which rises hundreds of feet in the air over the District of Columbia, and is dedicated to our first President If you were to climb the stairs of the Washington Monument you would read the following words "God and our native land," "'The memory of the just is blessed:' Proverbs 10:7," "Search the Scriptures," "Holiness to the Lord," "Suffer the little children to come unto me and forbid them not; for of such is the kingdom of God," "Train up a child in the way he should go; and when he is old, he will not depart from it," "In God we trust," "May heaven to this union continue its beneficence." If you were able to get to the top of the Washington Monument on the outside, you would read on that metal cap these engraved words "Praise be to God."

If you were then to visit that repository of the greatest collection of human knowledge ever amassed in one place by living human beings, the Library of Congress, and if you were to note carefully the walls of the various rooms of that library, you would see such sentiments as these: "The heavens declare the glory of God; and the firmament showeth His handywork," "Wisdom is the principal thing; therefore get wisdom; and with all thy getting, get understanding," "What doth the Lord require of thee, but to do justly, and to love mercy, and to walk humbly with thy God," "One God, one element, and one far-off divine event, to which the whole creation moves," "Nature is the art of God," and "That this nation, under God, shall have a new birth of freedom—and that government of the people, by the people, for the people, shall not perish from the earth."

If you were then moved in your heart, desirous to sing praises to God for what He has done in this your native land, you might lift up your voice with millions of others to sing the National Anthem of our country, *The Star Spangled Banner*, which concludes with these words:

Praise the Power that hath made and preserved us a nation!
Then conquer we must, when our cause it is just;
And the star-spangled banner in triumph shall wave
O'er the land of the free, and the home of the brave.

"A Time to Speak"

From our discoveries we realize that all the documents that formed our country, the ideals of those who framed them, the convictions of those who settled this land, all the Constitutions of the various states, the inaugurals of all our presidents, the statements on all the monuments, unmistakably testify that this is a nation under God founded for the furtherance of the Gospel and Kingdom of our Lord Jesus Christ.

Those are but a few of hundreds of examples that could be mentioned. On them I rest my case. Again I ask you, does the separation of church and state mean that God isto have no place in our land? Does it mean that this nation was not founded for the glory of God and the advancement of the Kingdom of our Lord Jesus Christ, as has been repeatedly stated? Does it mean that Our government is to be secularist and humanist in nature? Does it mean that our children are to grow up without any knowledge of the God who brought about the founding of this country?

In 1929, the Communists issued a protocol which said that the concept of the separation of church and state should be pushed to the extremist position, that all religion should be removed as the underpinning for the government of this nation in order that, eventually having grown so weak and flabby and convictionless and fearful, this government might fall. We have moved a long way already on that path.

I believe that the time is long past for Christians to stand on their feet and say, "Thus far and no more!" and declare, as a decision of the Supreme Court has said, that this is a Christian land. All its documents, all its constitutions, and all the beliefs of its founders, indicate that this is true.

We must no longer tolerate the movement to reduce this nation to a secularistic, atheistic, humanistic state. My friend, are we to be spineless? Are we to allow these things to go on with out protest? Or are we to take steps as individual Christian citizens to see that the rights and privileges emanating from the free exercise of the religion which founded this nation are not abridged and expunged, as numerous efforts are now underway to do.

God grant that we may not be so weak, vacillating and fearful. May God grant us the courage to take our stand while there still is a place to make that stand.

May we pray:

Our Father, we thank Thee for those good and gracious men who came to this land, who left all behind and founded a new nation under God. We pray that Thou wilt forgive us that we have been so lax, that we have allowed things to go on without protest, without speaking our minds, without stating our opinions, without declaring the facts. Help us no longer to do so but in these critical days to make clear to this country that this nation was indeed founded under Thee. Bring us back. Bring a great revival to this land, we pray. And may Christian men and women assume the responsibilities of their Christian citizenship, that all that has been fought for and suffered for may not be lost by the apathy so prevalent in our midst. We pray this in the name of Jesus Christ Our Lord. Amen.

Dennis James Kennedy, better known as D. James Kennedy, was an American pastor, evangelist, and Christian broadcaster. He founded the Coral Ridge Presbyterian Church in Fort Lauderdale, Florida, where he was senior pastor from 1960 until his death in 2007. Kennedy also founded Evangelism Explosion International, Coral Ridge Ministries (since 2011, Truth in Action Ministries), the Westminster Academy in Fort Lauderdale, and Knox Theological Seminary.

Isis and the USA in Review

"How dreadful are the curses which Mohammedanism lays on its votaries! Besides the fanatical frenzy, which is as dangerous in a man as hydrophobia in a dog, there is this fearful fatalistic apathy. The effects are apparent in many countries. Improvident habits, slovenly systems of agriculture, sluggish methods of commerce, and insecurity of property exist wherever the followers of the Prophet rule or live. A degraded sensualism deprives this life of its grace and refinement; the next of its dignity and sanctity."

WINSTON CHURCHILL, THE RIVER

Note: *Churchill wrote this account of the campaign at Omdurman in Arabia in 1899 when he was still soldiering for the queen. It was his first major historical work and is still considered one of his most riveting.*

THE LIBRARY JOURNAL

ISIS and The USA in Review

Dr. Harry Reeder

The ISIS phenomena, Islamic terrorist attacks have occasioned an interesting response pattern from the administration of President Obama and even from him personally. There are doubtless multiple reasons as to why there is a hesitancy to identify the contemporary Jihadist movement as Islamic in both ideology and motivation. But whatever the reasons are, the fact is – our national leadership will, with both tortured rationalizations and inconsistencies, avoid labeling it as "Islamic" seemingly at all costs.

ISIS (Islamic State In al-Shama) is arguably the 7th Caliphate of Islam, an Islamic brand of theocracy that is determined to impress Sharia law upon the entire world. This movement is now spawning a Jihadist, terrorist, genocidal initiative against non-compliant Muslims, non-Muslims and other religions but, in particular, Jews and Christians. The focus upon Jews and Christians has been painfully obvious in recent attacks. But equally obvious was the resolute Administration's commitment to avoid identifying those targeted (Jews and Christians) or the terrorists (Islamic). In contrast the assailants publicly identified both themselves and the victims.

Recently in Paris a Jewish, kosher delicatessen was attacked. Four Jews were killed, and the perpetrator called a journalist to celebrate "killing some Jews." Yet, the President insisted on a veiled and incomplete assessment of the event as a "random act of despicable terror by an irrational religious death cult." While it was certainly "irrational" and "despicable" and it was the work of a "religious death cult," it was neither "random" nor was it just any "death cult." It, by the terrorists own affirmation, targeted Jews and was fundamentally rooted in a consistent and cleric-approved interpretation of the Quran by Muslim adherents of Islam.

More recently, ISIS Jihadists marched 21 Egyptian Christians, were in Libya to find work, onto a sandy Mediterranean beach. After verbally berating their captives and their Christianity, they ritually decapitated them because of their faith in Christ. Again, our President condemned the action by describing it as an "unspeakable act of barbarism upon Egyptian citizens." This, at best, is an incomplete assessment, not only ignoring the explanatory words of the Islamic Jihadists but also insinuating that these men were killed because they were "citizens of Egypt." Never mind the fact that all of these victims happened to be Christians on their knees calling upon Jesus to deliver them while being beheaded by self-identified Islamic Jihadists. Even still, our leaders would have us believe they were killed because they were Egyptian citizens at the hands of deranged cultists. These men were not only murdered because they were Christians. They were executed because they refused to recant their salvation, even though it might have saved them. Such disingenuous commentary upon their death dishonors them and makes the labeling of Maj. Nidal Hasan's killing spree in the name of Allah that produced 13 causalities at Fort Hood as "work place violence" almost plausible.

So why is our President doing this?

Honestly, I don't know for sure. I can only surmise five possibilities.

1. He personally senses or feels a need to protect the Islamic religion from being identified with the contemporary Islamic Jihadist Caliphate because of either its influence on him personally or perhaps family loyalty since he was raised in a family of professing Muslims. In other words,

because of his personal connection in the formative years of his live he has a desire to defend the religion he knew from being identified with embarrassing elements now identified with the religion.

2. He is concerned that he will offend (what we are told are the majority of Muslims) who reject this Caliphate Jihadist movement or at least its strategy and tactics.

3. He is concerned that Americans will be unable to discern between Jihadist Muslims and those Muslims who have rejected the current Caliphate or Holy War.

4. He, like the vast majority of Washington and the cultural elite, cannot believe that the Islamic religion could actually be the motivating and defining factor of those who are engaged in this genocidal Jihad. It is inconceivable to them that any religion could possibly matter that much to anyone. The fact is, those culturally committed to secular humanism find it unfathomable that religion could ever be a life and death issue to anyone.

My inclination is #4 but it could be none or some combination of any or all of them.

Some Unsolicited Advice

Mr. President, my unsolicited advice is this: If you either sympathize or personally desire to honor the Muslim religion of your family, then simply tell us. But by the way, your recent apologetic on behalf of Islam to distance it from the self-identified Islamic Caliphate by illegitimately and inaccurately comparing it to the Crusades, may have been a brief but helpful insight as to your perspective on both Islam and Christianity. Or…

If you are concerned that an intellectually honest assessment of the ISIS-affirmed Islamic Caliphate will offend "peace loving Muslims" – then say so. As you do, you can call upon all "peace loving Muslims" to theologically, organizationally and politically police themselves and their religion. Throughout your Presidency you have displayed no hesitancy in telling Americans and/or Christians our perceived faults and how we need to correct ourselves relationally and socially for which, when accurate, we thank you. And it is distinctly possible that as you provide similar admonitions for the Muslim community perhaps they will also be grateful. Or…

If you are concerned that Americans will overreact and engage in wholesale persecution of all Muslims, then again say so and challenge us *not* to do so. Personally, given all that has happened since 9/11, I think you should be encouraged by the restraint of Americans and their overall consistently demonstrated desire to avoid overreaction and instead treat our Muslim neighbors with respect while affirming their First Amendment rights.

Finally, Mr. President, first, as a Christian and second, as a grateful American, my unsolicited advice and appeal is simple. I don't expect you to be an apologist for Islam. I am fully aware the Muslim religion has had an influential role in your life and you are adequately informed of its tenets and objectives. But you were not elected to evaluate whether a self-confessed Islamic Jihadist Caliphate is an authentic expression of their religion. You were elected to defend this country and its citizens "*from all enemies foreign and domestic.*" By the way, I do not expect you to be an apologist for Christianity either. You were not elected to be a Pastor or Imam but simply, yet profoundly, you were elected to be President of the United States and to fulfill your oath to protect us from avowed enemies. You need not evaluate the authenticity of the ideology or religion motivating those enemies – in this case whether their interpretation of Islam is valid or not. Simply protect the citizens of this nation – Christians, Jews, Muslims or atheists – who have been targeted in this state supported and religiously declared Holy War.

AN OVERVIEW

So exactly what is America facing? ISIS is the latest contemporary Muslim movement designed to impose Sharia Law through a world-wide Theocratic Fascist Islamic Caliphate. America is not faced with a "war on terror." Terror is a tactic of an unjust war not an enemy to defeat with war. Therefore this war is not against terror but Islamic terrorists. Our President is correct when he says we are not at war with Islam. We are at war with an Islamic Fascist Theocratic Caliphate affirmed by Muslim clerics who believe the Quran which teaches that those who do not convert and submit to Sharia Law in the name of Allah can be executed in a Holy War. In the Quran this doctrine is called "*Takfir*." But the result is whether we desire to acknowledge it or not they have embraced the practice of "*takfiri*" thereby declaring war on us.

It is a Caliphate. Al-Qaeda was not. It desired a Caliphate but could not declare one. ISIS can since a Caliphate requires both clerical authorization and a true state with boundaries to be authentic. ISIS has both. In fact, it occupies a land mass larger than the nation of Great Britain.

It is a Fascist movement. Fascism is a governmental system marked by centralization of authority employing governmental power to control and implement policies of suppression and marginalization of any opposition by coercion with economic, legal and if necessary, lethal power to achieve its objectives. Islam with its governmental enforcement of Sharia is Fascist.

It is a Theocratic religious movement defined by a historically consistent Islamic interpretation of the Quran, with an objective of a world-wide Islamic Caliphate or Apocalypse.

A FINAL WORD

Finally, to my Christian brothers and sisters in America – It is both righteous and faithful to God's Word for the President of the United States to use the power of the sword to protect us. Therefore, it is righteous and appropriate for our sons and daughters to give themselves to bear the sword of the State in a just defense of the country's citizens. In fact, the government's most important role, as defined by Scripture, is to serve as a minister of God to protect the lives of its citizens from any and all lethal aggression. The same text calls for us to both pray for our leaders and display respect for those who rule over us by God's sovereign hand (Rom. 13:1-7).

Furthermore, it is also right for us, as our Lord's church, to send our sons and daughters with the Sword of the Spirit and the Gospel to encourage

His people and to reach His enemies. While remembering we too, were enemies of Christ when the Gospel came to us through His people proclaiming Jesus who will redeem His enemies and bring them into His family by delivering us from sin's deception and power as well as its guilt and shame. All of this is made possible because of His atoning death upon the Cross and His triumph over the grave.

So, Mr. President, respectfully we are praying for you. And our sons and daughters are ready to protect and serve the citizens of this country with the Sword of the State in a just war.

And, to our enemies, we are also sending our sons and daughters with the "Weapons of the Spirit" protected by the "Armor of Christ" as "sheep to be slaughtered." They come with the Sword of the Spirit – the Word of Truth – so that you may be set free from sin and fear. We long for you to hear the Spirit of God say "Come," and the Bride of Christ – His Church – say "Come." As we heard Christ, we pray you will also. We go to you so that you might hear the Gospel, His glorious message of salvation by grace and "come to Christ" – the King who died and is risen so that we who were His enemies – helpless and hopeless – might have life forevermore – *"Come."*

Dr. Harry L. Reeder, III serves as senior pastor of the 4,000-member Briarwood Presbyterian Church, birthplace of the PCA denomination. As a pastor/teacher, his philosophy of ministry is drawn from Ephesians 4:11–16: he is called to "equip the saints" to do "the work of the ministry." Beyond Briarwood, Pastor Reeder teaches leadership courses through Reformed Theological Seminary and mentors graduating seminarians as pastoral fellows.

Pastor Reeder also has radio programs aired all throughout the southeast, started the "Embers to a Flame" ministry at Briarwood, and a follow ministry "Fanning the Flame." Pastor Reeder is the author of From Embers to a Flame: How God can Revitalize Your Church *(P&R Publishing, 2004) among other published articles and works.*

Reeder is a graduate of Covenant College, with a degree in history and Bible. He holds a Master of Divinity degree from Westminster Seminary and a Doctor of Ministry degree from Reformed Theological Seminary. He has previously served three churches as Senior Pastor, including Pinelands Presbyterian Church in Miami, Florida and Christ Covenant Presbyterian in Charlotte, North Carolina, which providentially grew from 38 to 3,000 in attendance under his shepherding.

A Parable

First they came for the Socialists, and I did not speak out—
Because I was not a Socialist.
Then they came for the Trade Unionists, and I did not speak out—
Because I was not a Trade Unionist.
Then they came for the Jews, and I did not speak out—
Because I was not a Jew.
Then they came for me—and there was no one left to speak for me.

MARTIN NIEMÖLLER

A Parable

by Paula Rodriguez

Once upon a time there was a sleepy little village. Some of the homes had been there a very long time, and some were brand new. The citizens of the village had formed a volunteer fire department to protect their homes. They met once a month to talk about things like fire drills, fire safety inspections, and to reminisce about the good old days in the village.

Because they wanted to know as soon as there was a fire, they hired a fire chief. The fire chief hired an assistant and then appointed a committee to be in charge of fire safety. The chief agreed to notify the villagers immediately if there were any fires, but they really did not expect to have any because the people of the village were so very careful.

One day, though, an old abandoned house in the center of the village burned down. When the villagers asked the chief why had hadn't called them, he said, "I met with my assistant and the fire safety committee. We agreed that the house was old and falling down anyway, so I thought it would be a waste of your time to try to save it." So the people of the village felt better, knowing that the chief had everything under control, and went back to their homes.

Some time later, another house burned down, then another, and another. Each time the chief explained why he had not called the villagers—there was a poor foundation, cracks in the walls, etc. He told them to trust him--that he knew what was best and that he would definitely call them if they were needed.

One day a strange report began to circulate among the villagers. One of the citizens claimed to have seen the chief standing by watching while a house burned to the ground. The villagers immediately went to the chief and asked him about this rumor, but he assured them that it wasn't true. "Just trust me," he said. "I have your best interests at heart. I will protect you. Don't worry. Just leave everything to me." So the villagers felt better knowing that they could trust the chief and his committee to do what needed to be done.

Finally one day a brand new house burned to the ground. The villagers saw the smoke and ran to the scene. They arrived to see the house in flames and the chief, his assistant, and the committee watching from a distance.

"What's going on here?" they asked.

"The committee has investigated, and there were a lot of things wrong with the house," said the chief, "and it had to go."

"But that's not true," said the people of the village. "We've been in that house many times. We watched it being built, and it was almost flawless. Why did you let it burn?"

"Don't worry about it," said the chief. "There are things that you don't know. Just trust me and my committee. We will do what's best for you."

So the people left everything in the hands of the chief and went back to their homes.

Not long after, the whole village burned to the ground. Now who is to blame for the loss of the village?

Paula Rodriguez is Chair of the Department of Speech Communication, Theatre, and Dance at Hinds Community College. She has been a member of the Presbyterian Church in America for over 40 years, and a pastor's wife for 32 of those years.

Book Review

"But since we have learned sin, we have found, as Lord Acton says, that 'all power corrupts, and absolute power corrupts absolutely.' The only remedy has been to take away the powers and substitute a legal fiction of equality."

C.S. Lewis

Book Review
Politics for Christians
by Francis J. Beckwith,
Intervarsity Press 2010

By Aaron Menikoff

Francis Beckwith is currently an associate professor of Church-State studies at Baylor University. In 2005 he was elected president of the Evangelical Theological Society. Two years later, he converted to Roman Catholicism and resigned. With degrees in philosophy and law, Beckwith has written a great deal on the nexus between church and state.

Politics for Christians (part of IVP's Christian Worldview Integration Series) is written for college students. "My purpose," writes Beckwith, "is to introduce the college student to politics by way of a few issues and questions that should be of concern to contemporary Christian citizens in liberal democracies" (39).

In these pages, Beckwith argues that because morality is at the heart of society, explicitly Christian arguments should be made and welcomed in the public sphere. After an introductory chapter examining what it means to study politics, Beckwith gets to the meat of the book. First, he argues that Christians are obligated to work for the common good. In that sense, they should be Christian citizens. Second, he argues that the First Amendment is in place to protect religious liberty, which includes granting Christians the freedom to make a religious case for their policy views. Third, Beckwith argues that there is no such thing as a neutral state. Advocates of secular liberalism are, in reality, sectarian since secular liberalism "presupposes and entails its own understanding of liberty and the human good that answer precisely the same philosophical questions that the so-called sectarian views answer" (143). This is a great chapter-clear, concise, helpful for someone tempted to leave faith out of policy decisions. Finally, he argues that the very existence of the "common good" is overwhelming evidence for the existence of God.

Like Richard John Neuhaus in *The Naked Public Square*, Beckwith helpfully strips away the misguided notion that religious motivations ruin the intellectual credibility of political and legal arguments. Furthermore, he is right to call for an integration of these two spheres since, as Don Carson has shown in *Christ and Culture Revisited*, Christians particularly struggle to understand what faith means for life outside the four walls of the church meeting-house. Finally, given how many books are pushing Christians into social activism-Kathleen Kennedy Townsend, *Failing America's Faithful* (Warner Books, 2007); E. J. Dione Jr., *Souled Out* (Princeton, 2008); Jim Wallis, *The Great Awakening* (Harper One, 2008)-it is nice to have a work pressing young people to defend the sanctity of marriage and every human life.

Still, I have two concerns.

First, it is not sufficient to argue, as Beckwith does, that Christians deserve a hearing in the public square. At the dawn of American history, most Christians did not have to fight to be heard. Society welcomed a Christian worldview. There was general agreement that for America to succeed (politically, economically, socially) it needed to be virtuous and, to be virtuous, America needed a religious foundation. "America" was not the king or the president, but the people. This explains why, printed outside the governor's office in the Oregon State Capitol, could be found words that may seem out of place today:

In the souls of its citizens will be found the likeness of the state which if they be unjust and tyrannical then will it reflect their vices but if they be lovers of righteousness confident in their liberties so will it be clean in justice, bold in freedom.

Rarely will the policies of a nation rise above the standards of the people. Even if Christians win that hearing in the public square, of what good will it be unless the citizens themselves are "lovers of righteousness"? If the Christian college students of today are going to be the leaders of tomorrow, they have to deal with this question. Some of the most important avenues of political activism have very little to do with the Supreme Court and everything to do with the court of public opinion. To my regret it is a topic that Beckwith either ignored or, more likely, deemed outside the purview of his project. Nonetheless, I think it is an issue that must be dealt with in an introduction to politics written for Christians.

Second, Beckwith underestimates or assumes the power of the gospel to change lives and world-views. This is a dangerous omission. At the heart of Christian action-whether it is social, political, or economic-is the gospel. A person is changed by the redeeming work of Jesus Christ. Such a change is the work of the Holy Spirit wrought in the heart of one who repents and believes the gospel (Mark 1:15; 1 Peter 2:24). Society may change as a result of this personal transformation, but there is no guarantee that one conversion or even an amalgamation of conversions will reform political or social structures, laws, policies, executive orders, etc. But it is good and godly to try!

But Beckwith appears unconvinced that the gospel is *first and foremost* about personal salvation. After describing several texts that do indeed demand sacrifice and mercy on the part of believers, he reaches this stunning conclusion: "It seems then that the Christian gospel is as much about getting heaven into people as about getting people into heaven" (66). I want to be sympathetic. Beckwith simply wants us to understand that Christians must engage the world. The Bible demands it. Yet, the implications of broadening the definition of the gospel to include "getting heaven into people" will ultimately harm political activism. Political movements that fail to gain traction may lead some to think the gospel has failed. What happens if same-sex marriage is legalized in every state, and if abortion continues to be protected? [This article was written prior to the of 2015 the Supreme Court decision declaring same-sex marriage legal in all states. However, God's law of one man and one woman in marriage still stands, is superior to the Supreme Court decision, and must be honored by every Christian] Has the gospel failed? Of course not! But this is because the gospel is *not* about getting heaven into the people and *is* about getting people into heaven. Beckwith does not make this clear and in a book entitled, *Politics for Christians*, he should.

Let me be clear. I am very thankful for men and women who promote the common good regardless of their motivation. But motivation is important, and a work entitled *Politics for Christians* should make it clear how the gospel relates to Christian citizenship. Otherwise, it might as well be called *Politics for Everyone*.

Originally published by Gospel Coalition Book Reviews, June 23, 2011

Aaron Menikoff (PhD, The Southern Baptist Theological Seminary) is senior pastor of Mt. Vernon Baptist Church in Atlanta, Georgia, and author of Politics and Piety *(Pickwick. 2014). Before pastoral ministry, he served as an aide to United States Senator Mark O. Hatfield.*